Single,
but Not Alone

SINGLE BUT NOT ALONE

ELLEN WEBER

BROADMAN PRESS
Nashville, Tennessee

© Copyright 1990 ● Broadman Press
All rights reserved
4253-47
ISBN: 0-8054-5347-4
Dewey Decimal Classification: 305.3
Subject Heading: SINGLE PEOPLE
Library of Congress Catalog Card Number: 89-29552
Printed in the United States of America

Unless otherwise stated, all Scripture quotations are from the Holy Bible, *New International Version,* copyright © 1973, 1978, 1984 by International Bible Society.

Scripture quotations marked KJV are from the King James Version of the Bible.

Scripture quotations marked RSV are from the *Revised Standard Version of the Bible,* copyrighted 1946, 1952, © 1971, 1973.

Scripture quotations marked TLB are from *The Living Bible.* Copyright © Tyndale House Publishers, Wheaton, Illinois, 1971. Used by permission.

Scripture quotations marked Phillips are reprinted with permission of MacMillan Publishing Co., Inc., from J. B. Phillips: *The New Testament in Modern English,* Revised Edition. © J. B. Phillips 1958, 1960, 1972.

Library of Congress Cataloging-in-Publication Data

Weber, Ellen, 1946-
    Single, but not alone / Ellen Weber.
      p. cm.
    ISBN 0-8054-5347-4
    1. Single parents—Prayer-books and devotions—English.   2. Single people—Prayer-books and devotions—English.   I. Title.
BV4596.S48W43   1990
242'.64—dc20   89-29552
                                               CIP

To
My dear friend
Pearl Kingsfield,
whose faithfulness and encouragement
over many years contributed to this book.

CONTENTS

Foreword

In the "good old days" to be a single parent was unique. Today, it is the lot for scores of millions. For these single parents and for all who find themselves alone, *Single, but Not Alone* is a much-needed, very practical book. It says in a million ways no matter how far down you slip, God will never let go. This is the very real journey Ellen Weber took. But more than her own wanderings, this book tells the story of God's faithfulness. Here is a handbook of hope; a help to others who feel broken or are experiencing the sudden shock of a lonely place. It takes a flight over the problem and shouts, "Hold on! God loves you." *Single, but Not Alone* is not just a specialty book. It meets a universal need. If you are a human being, it's just the book for you.

Harald Bredesen
Escondido, California

Introduction

Just the thought of starting another day made me pound the snooze button in an attempt to avoid meeting its pressures. My routines as a high-school teacher and single parent grew into a monster out to get me.

"I quit!" I shouted to Minew, our faithful tabby, because there was nobody else around. Min yawned and asked to be let out.

"But there must be another side to being a single parent," I protested, opening the door.

It was worth an investigation. After slipping into a few ruts and falling over several cliffs, I decided to hang glide over my toughest areas and take another look. To my surprise, life seemed much more exciting from my new position above the dilemmas and mundane routines.

Having tried everything else, I now climbed onto eagle wings and took in the whole scene. This book is the picture of 12 years as single parent, viewed from my new perspective. Some of the stories are funny, some miraculous, but all are true.

Oh yes, there were distractions calling out false solutions from every corner of my broken world. Often the forest got lost in the tundra I slogged through. And I sometimes felt like one of the tiniest Lilliputians with Gulliver, my unleashed giant enemy.

Personal columns told me to sign up with their friendly computors. Then Romeo, they promised, would drop from the clouds to whisk us away in his golden chariot. Television ads said: "Buy more clothes; put streaks in your hair." The cults wanted any extra money we had toward a little "security." The great halls of learning screamed: "Get more education!" And lottery booths sang, "For just a little, you can win a fortune." At times I listened.

But a few excursions on these tracks assured me there were no pots of gold at the ends of these counterfeit rainbows. The false roads did start me looking, though. And God's love and mercy along the way pointed to building blocks I would have otherwise ignored in my search for our security called "home." God's persistent love ended my search. He was so gentle and patient along the way, gripping my hand, and planting my feet on firm paths. He opened my eyes to see beauty all around me; He healed my broken heart. I write this book convinced that single parents have a special place in His most intimate love.

Not that it was always a breeze. Nor is it easy to be a child in a single-parent home. But there are answers! When I faced the responsibility head-on, refused to jump on the bandwagons of guilt or self-pity or blame others for our state, our new foundations began.

I don't pretend to have all the answers. Still, I can honestly say that the past 12 years have been filled with fun and challenges as Tanya and I took God's hand and followed down His path for our single-parent life. Highlights from our journey fill the pages of this book. If even one experience from our story makes your load a little lighter or adds a chuckle to your way, it will have been worth writing. And I fully expect that God will encourage you as He did us as you go. Perhaps you can glean encouragement even from our mistakes.

Today, at 14, Tanya scores high in her ninth-grade curriculum. She has known for four years that God is calling her to be a doctor on the mission fields. We both feel confident that in leading her there, He will give us every tool we need to build foundations toward that end. His perfect faithfulness over the past 12 years proves His care. So we both trust easier.

That is why we can shout for joy and invite others, who are "single but not alone," to come with us.

Each chapter includes a Bible passage for thought or discussion. There is a list of questions at the end of each, for personal follow-up or group Bible studies.

1
God's Perspective on a Thing

"It is just as important to sing about beautiful mornings as it is to talk about slums," Oscar Hammerstein said. I have often added: it is just as important to laugh at the lighter side of a thing as it is to deal with the pressures.

How one looks at a situation usually determines how successfully one tackles it. Whenever I worried about my future as a single parent, I saw all my own inadequacies. These often condemned me. But then I stumbled into another formula that lifted me above the pressures. It was simply this: when I looked up to God and asked for His heart on the matter, I moved ahead. It never failed. As a matter of fact, I found that without exception, God's perspective on a thing lifted me up.

One day I was preparing a banquet for the adult Bible school, which I direct at my church. Long days and nights went into the plans. Sometimes we left the church after midnight. Many telephone calls had to be made. Last-minute details kept me at the church most of the last day, leaving no time to prepare a thing to wear. I was tired, and tables for 100 guests still needed to be set.

"Lord," I prayed, "You know all about this, so I leave it all to You." With just an hour left til the guests arrived, I dashed home to change. There I found a new mohair sweater especially knit for me. My dear friend Dick, a retired doctor, had started the pullover two years earlier and finished it that day. He did not even know about the banquet. But God did! And He heard my prayer. Dick's daughter, Jenny, loaned me a coral skirt that picked up the peach flecks in my sweater for a perfect match. I felt so loved, the ache in my feet faded. The Lord took care of every detail. This is just one small example of how His love reaches down in practical ways.

All evening I felt like a princess because of my regal gift from God. Then when we drove home exhausted at 11:30 p.m. There was a bouquet of flowers by the door. They were left earlier in the day by a couple I had helped weeks before. The flower shop phoned this couple on the day before to apologize for the mix-up. So my friends approved the new delivery date: today! God's timing was perfect! How particular the Lord is to express love to us when we trust Him and look up. It often comes when we least expect it. An amazing thing about divine love—we never have to earn it, just accept it.

Often I shut His love out by entertaining negative thoughts. It took years and one dear friend who cared and always believed in me, to point this out. "You have to say no to the flesh and yes to the Spirit," he would say every time I hit bottom. Not many people will be able to speak truth even when it hurts and then stand by while you assimilate it. But when God sends such a friend, he or she is closer than a brother. God will send His own closest friends along to bring His love just at the point when we need it most. Only such a friend can enter into a person's life and see the obstacles through another's eyes.

Not that it's easy to be positive when things are tough and you are alone. It comes more from knowing who God is than from trying to get positive feelings about a thing. Many professionals have working formulas to positive attitudes today. But Corrie Ten Boom comes to mind when I think of *positive*. Her way leaves the professionals behind much like the donkey Jesus rode left the Cadillac driven by a Pharisee behind. When trouble struck, Corrie lost her thoughts in Jesus' love for her. When she was humiliated and her sister pushed into death in a Nazi German concentration camp, where they were taken for helping Jews, she meditated on Jesus' compassion and love for her.

Not that opposition flees instantly every time. The devil will try to drag you into fear and despair. Remember he is sometimes an angel of light. That's why a person needs God's perspective. Not that it won't try you. Just the opposite. But react in God's way, and you will be surprised how strong you get.

In the first few months I was left alone I heard noises at night that often woke me from a deep sleep. One night I was desperate. I crawled out of bed and scrambled for my Bible more out of fear than any real hope of finding deliverance. Being too afraid to turn the lamp on, I read through Jehoshaphat's fear in 2 Chronicles, chapter 20, using a flashlight. Something happened to me that turned fear into faith at 3:30 A.M. It was more than just identifying with Jehoshaphat's dilemma, or the comfort that comes when you see a Bible character confront your own fears. God somehow uses His Word to help you through. It's hard to explain exactly how Jehoshaphat became a real person right there to bring the answer. Something just snapped my fear, and I knew that God moved on my behalf. The next thing I knew, it was six o'clock. My alarm reminded me that I had fallen fast asleep as if the noises had never come.

Not only do fear and discouragement set in more easily to the single parent, but doubt will rob your peace, if you let it. Remember, the devil may go about as a roaring lion, but before the Lord he's toothless. When I saw God's perspective, I thanked Him for helping me. The noises stopped as abruptly as they came and have never returned. Once you forget who comforts in your trouble and whose love never fails, you are discouragement's prey. But there are answers.

Watch for the traps. Sickness, for example, can tear your eyes off the Lord and onto your troubles. I was hit with intense back spasms a few years ago. "You're pulling a load that was never meant for your back," my doctor warned. I simply refused to listen to the warnings my back sent out.

Report cards had to be into the office in two days, and I was still grading English projects for my senior classes. Tanya had outgrown most of her clothes and needed new ones. The house looked like a bulldozer had gone berserk in it, and the freezer was empty. Bible college pulled me away three nights a week. Only years later did I see God's perspective. I was heading for crisis, and my Father knew it. So He stepped in before I hit bottom.

I bent over to pick up a pen in my classroom and couldn't get up again. The spasms in my back rippled up and down like electric currents surging through the muscles. I called good friends, and they brought me to their home 20 minutes later. For one month I lay in bed too ill to even get to the doctor's office. For the first week I just slept as long as the injections loosened the spasms. I knew I had smashed through my tolerance barriers and would have to wait out the repairs. But God met me in that month and restored my health. More important, He gave me His perspective on my hurdles.

My biggest battles came from within. As I lay in bed, unable to move a finger, I remembered hurts I had met in the past. Instead of forgiving and going on, I had tried new ways to handle them better. The next step was always to condemn myself for not reacting in a godly way. And I judged others! Often the argument went on for hours in my own mind. And I allowed activity to crowd out the work God wanted to do in my heart.

But the Lord was gracious. Through all the hurdles of self, He showed me how to meditate in His word and get my eyes on Him instead of failure. There were many times around that mountain for me. Each time, I asked, "Forgive me, Lord, for forgetting You and looking at my own weaknesses." He knows our frame and shows mercy to forgive; no matter how often we fall, His love wins us back.

I remember one night kneeling beside the bed and pouring out to the Lord a major hurt that still throbbed. After I spouted every detail and complained bitterly about the hoplessness of it all, I heard a gentle whisper to my heart, and I knew it was God.

"Ellen, I love you!"

That was all it took. Love covers every other thing. Hurts flee in love's wake. I had no quarrel with any of the details anymore. The assurance of God's love is enough to keep one pressing on toward His complete healing. My whole being was filled with the warmth of His care and love. Nothing else mattered.

That experience taught me a principle. When I am aware of God's love for me, I can sing my way through the tough places.

Near the end of that month I took the plunge out of teaching and into writing full-time. I had to give notice and go back to finish the year, but God confirmed over and over that He would take me through. And He did.

Although she rarely complained, Tanya had needs that I couldn't see when I was discouraged about our situation. Over the years I see many children ignored while single parents try to re-build on the sands of false hopes and dreams. When I am downcast, I am like a condemned building, no good except to stand and wait to be torn down.

But we are capable of more! And our children are quite able, with God's help, to bring their own love into a home. They can be part of the very tool God uses to pick up the pieces and rebuild.

Recently, I drove through the epidemic slums in Chicago. The experts are now saying there might not really be any answers to the problem of thousands of children being born out of wedlock every year. It seems that one of the status symbols among gangs there is to father children illegitimately. The young boys apparently seek their pleasures in bringing more children into their own miserable lives to score a notch with their peers.

Without God there is no hope for the single-parent home. But with Him every one of our children has a chance to be whole. Faith can do even more. It can restore all the lost beauty and rehabilitate the abused and neglected child. Faith does not depend on my ability. It is divine, drawing from the perfect faithfulness of God given to me as a free gift. If I believe, it becomes mine. But I need to draw close to God to understand how to use faith.

Praying with an open mind helped me to get God's perspective on my day. Then I would take short, meaningful passages of scripture and chew on them until they penetrated my mind. I made a point of telling God how much I loved Him to replace thoughts of unworthiness or loneliness. I often thought of the words in Isaiah 26:3:

> You will keep in perfect peace
> him whose mind is steadfast,
> because he trusts in you.

Robert A. Russell wrote:

How did man get out of the Kingdom of God? How did he lose his place in it? By his negative thinking. How does he return to it? How can he find expression in a Kingdom of God only? By using the mind of Christ, by allying his thoughts with the Divinity within him. If we are praying or speaking the word for some greater good, we know that Christ is speaking the word through us. "In all thy ways acknowledge Him, and He shall direct thy paths." "Delight thyself also in the Lord; and He shall give thee the desires of thine heart."[1]

There are certainly many things one could be glum about, and the habit grows fast for the parent who now carries all the burdens —even those meant to be shared. But God has never yet turned His back on anyone who came to Him for strength. So remain positive, and you'll walk through. He carries those burdens too big for your shoulders and offers you His rest instead. What a trade!

Psalm 68 shows God to be my Father and Husband. When I read the psalm I set out with a new determination to allow God these places in my heart. As He became my All in all, a new joy sang His love tunes in my life!

Ralph Spalding Cushman shared how we can all run to Him for safety, in our times of trouble, in a poem he called "The Secret."

> I met God in the morning
>   When my day was at its best,
> And His presence came like sunrise,
>   Like a glory in my breast.
>
> All day long the Presence lingered,
>   All day long He stayed with me,
> And we sailed in perfect calmness
>   O'er a very troubled sea.
>
> Other ships were blown and battered,
>   Other ships were sore distressed,
> But the winds that seemed to drive them
>   Brought to us a peace and rest.
>
> Then I thought of other mornings,
>   With a keen remorse of mind,
> When I too had loosed the moorings,
>   With the Presence left behind.
>
> So I think I know the secret,
>   Learned from many a troubled way:
> You must seek Him in the morning
>   If you want Him through the day! [2]

Bible Study Suggestions

2 Chronicles 20

Practical Applications

1. How did Jehoshaphat feel when they reported a great multitude was coming against him?

2. How did he handle the situation?

3. How did Jehoshaphat comfort himself in the crisis?

4. What is the hardest situation for you right now?

5. Consider these five qualities of God that show His delivering power through your situation.

- Psalm 147:5:
- Exodus 13:21:
- Nehemiah 9:19:
- Psalm 31:3:
- 1 Samuel 2:3:

Notes

1. *You Try It* (Marina del Ray: De Vorss and Co., 1953).
2. *Spiritual Hilltops* (Nashville: Abingdon-Cokesbury Press, 1932).

2
My Father's Definition of Me

One van Gogh painting reportedly sold for $40 million. Yet there are five billion people in this world, each one a creative masterpiece of the Most High God. How much more than a van Gogh each person is.

You may feel like anything but a masterpiece. I struggled for years with an inner war after I faced life alone. After all, who leaves behind a masterpiece? you may ask. Over and over, I begged God to show me His perspective. The fact is: God has defined each one. Not only that, He thought so much of you He bought you with His Son's life. So why not ask His definition of you.

My problem was not so much with God's silence but with my hearing. It took years for the Word to renew my thinking so that I saw myself as God did. But I finally did grasp God's view. And with my knowledge came an amazing strength to look more to God instead of my own inadequacies. The result? A peace which no crisis can destroy.

I heard two Christians talking while they wrapped parcels together on a long counter at a business near my home. One middle-aged woman said to the other well-dressed lady in her fifties. "Here, let me help you. You must be desparate." The older woman snapped back, "Look, I'm not desperate, OK? I'm a Christian, and Christians never get desperate!" I wanted to swing around from the card stacks and yell, "I get desperate sometimes!"

Why do we wear masks? Why do we hide from one another?

Have you ever longed to unmask the ones around you, so you could be simply you? Achievement is emphasized today. Who can be the best? But in a person's climb to the top of success's ladder, he too often defines himself by the grades obtained. Or worse, he demands perfection from everybody around because he refuses to look at the unyielded areas of a hardened heart. Be careful you don't get too mature. Or do you ever feel you have to look spiritual so others will think you are? You flee from love every time you set walls up. And it's lonely inside.

Someone asked a pastor of a growing and dynamic church how he did it. The pastor replied: "I hold a crown a few inches above my people's heads and watch them grow into it."

What a picture of Jesus' way with each one of us. He holds a perfect crown up and gives everything we need to grow into it. Then He gives us the crown for growing. His love produces love in us. His faith produces faith; His trust, trust. Jesus sees us not as we are but as we can become.

But did you ever ask, "Who am I?"

Or worse, did you ever define yourself by your ability to do something? You may win a few scores, but you hit bottom every time.

What more sinking feeling can you get than when you blow it and lose a dear friend's love. Or how often have you ever grieved because you used a friend or broke a confidence. Not that you have to stay down. As soon as we ask, God forgives and then forgets. But the relationship between you and that person may take years to mend.

Not so with God! Once we are born again, we are His. And God's love never lets you go. Remember, He loves you with a perfect love just the way you are. The height of God's love was set at Calvary. So no matter how many times I slip, His love remains the same. *When God looks at you He sees His Own Son, Jesus.* You and I are covered with the blood of Jesus. That makes us perfectly loved.

Then why do so few feel loved?

Our culture conditions us to earn love. In kindergarten you get a smile when you sit quiet and a reprimand when you talk out. As you go on in school, you compete for math marks, spelling bees, volleyball teams, and eventually a date for Saturday night. You cram for entrance exams to college, and the marks to stay there. Work, work, work! When you win, you feel good about who you are. But what about when you lose?

Why look for some outside influence to make you feel good about who you are? If you find yourself waiting for the mail each day or standing in lottery lines for a windfall, you may be handing over your worth to a faulty receiver. Only God's love will sweep away that emptiness you feel inside.

Only when you recognize who you really are can you find wholeness. Once you do, start living like the child of the King. I heard a story long ago that I've never forgotten. An eagle's egg fell from the nest and hatched with a dozen chicks. That little bald eagle scratched around the barnyard for chicken feed like the chickens did. Then one day a great bald eagle flew overhead. The bird soared directly overhead one minute, then beat the winds of the upper air the next. The little bird flapped his wings for the first time. After a few trial runs he took flight. No longer would he peck the ground with chickens. He belonged to the noblest of all birds.

You were born to soar like the eagle. Think of it! Made in God's Own image: His child. But there is one condition. You have to claim your divine heritage before you own it.

Other people all do something well, and what can I do? you may ask. Remember God gives gifts to every one of us. Only you have special ability to do some particular thing for God. Don't compare your gift with another person's. You are unique.

Hard work may be required to develop that gift. But as you grow, your sense of purpose will spur you on. It is not that persons earn love from God by exercising their gifts. Nor is heaven earned. Your sense of well-being is heightened when you are fulfilling the divine call of God for you. A dear friend once explained it this way, "You are the Ellen expression of Christ. There will never be another one."

It makes sense. We are all different. Your background gives you unique traits. Your family, education, Christian experience, place of birth, and position in the community—all make you, you. Add God's call for your life, and you have a specially designed destiny to look forward to. One that starts now!

Think of it! When God considered His highest dreams for creation, you were there.

> For I know the plans I have for you, says the Lord. They are plans for good and not for evil, to give you a future and a hope (Jer. 29:11, TLB).

I was born in the middle of a family of seven kids in Nova Scotia. I was 14, when my mother died of cancer. Life fell apart at that time. Somehow I managed to hold together and "get ahead" until I became 29. That year the entire bottom dropped out. Alone, I wondered how I could possibly bring up a toddler myself.

I was sure it was all over. Many days I was so far down I had to look up to see bottom. Then Tom, my brother, and his wife, Dolores, showed me how God turned their lives around. That night I gave my heart to the Lord. On September 13 of that year, I asked God to take over, and I've never looked back.

Happiness did not follow me every day. But where I was shattered, I'm now whole. Where I was confused, I enjoy peace today. And I have a secure purpose for the first time. God may mold and shape you with the skill of the finest craftsman, but His love will never let you go!

Relationships came together after years of walled silence. And through it all I recognized the urgency of the words *know thyself.* In order to know who you are, you have to know God first. Knowing God comes by belief and acceptance.

Remember, you are redeemed with royal blood. God's love for

you was expressed in its highest form at Calvary. In other words, Jesus loved you personally enough to die. Nothing more can increase that love. Calvary bought you at the highest price possible. But how does that affect who I am? you may ask. The answer spun my own life around 180 degrees. Here it is. You cannot earn God's love, though many still try. God doesn't love you one degree less, for example, when you forget to pray or study His word. His love is set at the top of the scale by the sacrifice at the cross. When you rest in this fact, you begin to enjoy God. You accept His love and love Him back.

Now, instead of the harshness of the Law driving you, you begin to live like the child of the King. Not that we don't fail and let God down. He knows our frailty. But His love never fails, never turns away. It doesn't change either. And God's love will call a person to repentance faster than any law.

I once saw a book called: *It's Not My Business What You Think of Me*. That's true. But others do confirm who we are. If you speak well, somebody will usually invite you again. Even then, don't be bound by other's opinions.

Early in my Christian walk, God seemed to impress me to pray about my speaking rather than offer to speak anywhere. And I do. Then for some reason, a few years ago, the Lord put almost all my speaking on the shelf for three years. Nobody invited me to speak. But I had peace. As a matter of fact, other areas came alive in my ministry, and my writing took on many new dimensions at that time. God knows best. One thing I did notice. By the time speaking invitations came again, I loved writing and no longer enjoyed teaching as much. Even after I had taught high school for 20 years, God changed my directions.

I look to God for guidance, but others influence my ministry. Some churches ask me to speak, and I do. Others say: women must not speak, and I don't. It's really up to God. Ever since He asked me not to volunteer, He manages my time.

People who don't know who they are, lack peace. They may go

on endless binges of self-denial, striving, or confession. But they are running the race in a maze of confusion. They may not recognize it at first. I hid quite well behind my walls of insecurity.

No one lacks a need for acceptance. Denial of affection obstructs the deepest human need. And the converse is true. Without somebody's approval our confidence shrinks. And with it the courage to try again.

Once, however, you discover God's perspective of you, even criticism becomes easier to take. And let's face it. We all get criticized. But if a sharp word knocks you down, check your position in God. A perfectly loved child of the King bounces back faster than an orphan.

Where you once defended yourself, you find you run to your Father, and He helps you through. Self-pity never becomes an option for the person hiding in God's refuge through a trial.

Remember, the most tender love of God often comes in the middle of a wilderness experience. Once you know without any doubt that God is for you, you can relax. Now you can enjoy God.

Years of counseling taught me that many Christians have picked up a distorted picture of God somewhere. Too many feel they have to please God—win His favor—before His love comes. Years of hard labor in hope of winning God's pleasure end in frustration and bitterness against God.

Why not just take God's word for who we are and then believe it? What a difference it makes. I used to thank God that He offered to be my Husband and Father and a Father to my daughter. My thanks brought faith to believe God for very practical expressions of a husband's and father's love. One morning Tanya and I prayed that God would show us a way to keep her in a Christian school. A few days later on the last day of school, the telephone rang. The school's secretary said, "A man just dropped by and paid Tanya's tuition for next year, Ellen." That man chose to remain anonymous. But we knew that Tanya's Father took care of her schooling. Since we've been on our own for many years with no help, we knew it was God's miracle gift. And many other crises found His extravagant provision. We thanked God more for His love toward us than the money it took to keep Tanya in school the next year.

I do not believe God always shows His love in material ways. He is a good Father, and He will provide whatever it takes to bring His child to maturity. Tanya is an honor student in that school today. She plans to study medicine and then work on the mission fields.

Once you look up and see God's thoughts about you, you care less what others think. But more important, you long to please the One who loves you with an unconditional love.

Bible Study Suggestions

Ephesians 1:3-14

Practical Applications

Read Ephesians 1:3-14 aloud replacing the first person plural with *I* or *me* to see who Christ made you.
It will read like this:

> Praise be to the God and Father of [my] Lord Jesus Christ, who has blessed [me] in the heavenly realms with every spiritual blessing in Christ. For he chose [me] in him before the creation of the world to be holy and blameless in his sight. In love he predestined [me] to be adopted as his [son/daughter] through Jesus Christ, in accordance with his pleasure and will—to the praise of his glorious grace, which he has freely given [me] in the One he loves. In him [I] have redemption through his blood, the forgiveness of sins, in accordance with the riches of God's grace that he lavished on [me] with all wisdom and understanding. And he made known to [me] the mystery of his will according to his good pleasure, which he purposed in Christ, to be put into effect when the times will have reached their fulfillment—to bring all things in heaven and on earth together under one head, even Christ.
>
> In him [I was] also chosen, having been predestined according to

the plan of him who works out everything in conformity with the purpose of his will, in order that [I, who was] the first to hope in Christ, might be for the praise of his glory. And you also were included in Christ when you heard the word of truth, the gospel of your salvation. Having believed, you were marked in him with a seal, the promised Holy Spirit, who is a deposit guaranteeing our inheritance until the redemption of those who are God's possession —to the praise of his glory.

1. What does it really matter who God says you are?

2. Why not list what God says He gave you in the passage above. Then thank Him.

3
What Others Think

Dr. Paul Brand, known for his work with lepers, told a story about John, a grotesquely misshapen leper. John walked into Brand's clinic in India. Brand went over and put an arm on the leper's shoulder and laughed. "I think we can get those hands working again," he said shaking a clawed hand. Tears ran down the leper's twisted face, and he mumbled something, but his whole mouth seemed to shift to one side. Brand asked the interpreter for help. "I wasn't laughing at him," the compassionate doctor explained.

"You didn't offend him. It's just that nobody has touched this man in 40 years," the interpreter told him.

Even after Brand cured the disease, its ugly deformities kept people away from John. Not that the leper helped. He agitated for strikes soon after an operation gave mobility to his rigid hands so he could work. Those strikes often found many followers. Everywhere the leper went, he caused trouble. John hated the world and had no use for God.

Brand's elderly mother, full of tender love and understanding for the poor, traveled some distance to help John. In just a few weeks he gave his heart to the Lord and turned around 180 degrees.

John had lived through so much rejection that he seemed unable to find acceptance and love. One day he challenged Brand, "You only love me because you're paid to. You have no choice. I am your patient. But I bet if I go to the village church, they won't accept me."

Brand visted the pastor. "I'll discuss your patient with our elders and get back to you," the pastor said. Brand assured him John was cured and could not pass leprosy on. It was agreed that John come that Sunday.

The two men walked in 10 minutes late and stood at the back of the packed church. All seats were full, men packed on one side, women on the other. Brand knew that unless John was welcomed he'd never return. But there were no seats!

Brandt felt desperate. A few people turned and looked at the man. Then an Indian six rows from the back turned and grinned. He placed two hands on the arm of the man beside him and shoved his whole row of men down. Then he patted the aisle seat next to him and motioned John to join him. "I could feel John's tense muscles against my arm loosen and relax," Brand said. He walked like a kid to the Christian man and sat down next to him.

After the service, Brand found John grinning ear to ear. "His life turned around like night to day at that moment," the doctor said. "He was never the same after that invitation."

The scars left on a single parent's heart may twist one's emotions like John's scars marred his body. But God sends others to bring back a sense of love and acceptance. Not that you wait for a Doctor Brand to come along. Just the opposite. Each one of us can light that single candle and have the joy of watching God restore somebody else. But the fact is: God sends others to fan His flames in a person's heart.

People walk into our world every day. A few of these will be friends and some just acquaintances. But there are others—the ones who come as pruning tools who are as significant to each one of us.

No one would deny we need each other. Yet which ones of us let our most essential lifelines slip away?

Sometimes the very person who clomps into your "vineyard" with the muddy cleats, squashing everything, does a deeper work in one's heart than a friend. I found, however, I had to take off my masks, rearrange my attitudes, and face myself honestly when my turf was threatened.

With no husband to provide for me, people walked in quite frequently and gave advice. Sometimes I didn't know whose advice to follow. I had to learn early in my walk to listen to God and follow Him. Then when I felt God called me to leave high-school teaching and write, a few eyebrows really raised. "How will you pay the rent?" some asked. "Nobody can make it as a writer," one journalist told me. And when I had no rent or no food for my daughter, I almost took their advice and quit.

I found such advice drove me deeper into God for its confirmation. Today's Christian writer needs tenacity; otherwise, we give the media over to the non-Christian by default. I prayed, "Father, so many leave this field through fear. Please tell me what to do." The key is to know God's call and then jump in boldly after it. When I looked at my directions through God's eyes, what a different view I got.

One woman in particular tried to discourage me from writing. "Are you working yet?" she asked me once when I met her on a walk. Once I yielded my heart to God and prayed for guidance, I began to look to the sun and face the storms with courage. Even when rejection slips came back I thanked God, fine-tuned that piece, and targeted it for another market.

It's not easy. I've all but given up at times. One guy sauntered up to me in the writing stacks at our library and shot out, "I'll bet your husband supports you while you sit and write romances." I smiled and said nothing. But inside I screamed, *I support my family on what my writing brings in.* Not that we've always made it. I've been so far down I had to look up to see bottom.

Those with nobody have it hardest. But God fights our battles when we follow Him. Remember, you are never alone. So many in my line of work have despaired, not knowing God. Oliver Gold-smith handed a manuscript to his furious landlady in 1762 while he drank away the woes of other debts. The manuscript *The Vicar of Wakefield* kept him going for a short while.

Let's face it: sheer determination often keeps our non-Christian colleagues going. How much more a Christian can look forward to. In 1605, the only home Cervantes could afford was a cot under the lamp on a staircase landing in a brothel. Every night sailors came through drunk. Footprints marred his pages, the ink got kicked over, and Cervantes even got beaten up. But the work went on.

While I have yet to write a *Don Quixote* or a *Vicar of Wakefield,* I've been encouraged by the tenacity of writers who went before me. But how much more encouraged is the writer who knows his Heavenly Father never sleeps. Remember, when those who oppose you step in, greet them as friends. Who knows what the Lord will do through them?

Did you ever start out with a friend and end up with a pruning knife. Or just the opposite—a person comes to oppose you, and you end up kindred spirits. Relationships are the only thing we can take with us to eternity. Look at all the deep friendships Jesus made in the few years of His life the Bible records. Notice the different kinds of people Jesus got to know on earth. What an example for us to be diversified in friendships. Those who look for only one kind of friend miss the chance to discover a treasure in somebody else. Why not pray and let the Lord bring His friends?

The woman at the well must have been shocked when Jesus spoke to her. Not only did men rarely speak to women in public but to be seen talking with a prostitute was unheard of. She came at noon. The others were having a rest, and she could get her water and sneak away unnoticed.

Did you ever want to steal away and hide somewhere? Maybe you've been with couples where a single doesn't really fit or with a family with no extra room for an outsider. More than once, when I have faced the aloneness of a single parent's walk I have been flooded with a sense of God's love.—That does not mean it's all easy sailing. Maybe your day was filled with giving out, and you're just drained. More than once I've dragged my tired feet back to our little apartment, assured that God's hand holds mine in these moments. And He never lets go! What a privilege!

Why not translate the trials you walked through into blessing for someone else. To begin you have to take your masks off. Then look at the toughest areas you ploughed through and make these a gift for at least one other person. Watch what happens.

Become a Friend

Although I had good friends before, my best friends today are people who came alongside when I hit bottom. There is always somebody who needs a friend if you're willing to be one. Don't always look in the obvious places. I discovered a few dear friends in my own church who felt desperately alone. Everyone of us has something to give to another person. That's a great start to a friendship.

Don't Give Quick Advice

Pete, a young father and widower, came to my home fellowship group one night and asked if he could join. Another Christian in his apartment block had discovered Pete drinking. Jim knew Pete was a Christian and that something was wrong. Jim invited Pete to the group. Pete told us, "They think it's my fault she died." Tears ran down his face.

Months passed before Pete opened up the real problem: his drinking. We explained to him what he already knew but refused to accept; his wife's cancer had nothing to do with his drinking. God cared about Pete and wanted to help him. Pete agreed to join Alcoholics Anonymous and get help with the two children.

Pete had big problems when he came. Years later I still thank God for the compassion for a broken man shown by that little group. Nobody started throwing answers at him. The group rallied around and helped this dear father pick up the broken pieces. What a blessing he is to that group today. You can always count on Pete to get a baseball game going. He laughs easily and often leads the Bible study.

Be There

Remember those times when the kids were tucked in and you faced the whole evening alone night after night? Remember how you wanted to share your concerns and miracles with somebody but felt the kids should be spared the emotional hurdles. So you had nobody to talk to.

When somebody drops by just as I'm about to begin an article on deadline, I sometimes remember one of my dearest friend's invitations. "Ellen, I always love to see you drop by anytime." And I knew she meant it. This woman kept busy and had too many commitments already. But she gave the most important gift a single parent could receive: "Drop in." And when I did, she acted as if a cup of coffee were all that was important to her at the time. Many an hour slipped by before I saw the love of Jesus wipe away those tears of loneliness.

You do encourage a person to abuse your time. But my friend's time was more the Lord's than her scheduled plans, so I never became a burden. And she often let me know that. One thing did happen in those months. A friendship cemented between us lasted years after the hurts fled. In fact, she is my dearest friend today.

Work One on One

We cannot take on a city but we can involve ourselves vulnerably with one or two single adults, resulting in a deep love and lasting friendship. Some churches build a program around people's needs from a family standpoint. Then when a holiday comes or tragedy hits, we get together with our friend. What a difference! Instead of dreading the day, as many I know still do, you come to look forward to a time with friends.

Walk Through What You Can, and Trust God for the Rest

You may think you have to restore the person God sends into your life. But you don't. Some people feel compelled to cure the sick. But that too is a myth. Remember Jesus tells us in Matthew 25 to *visit* the sick. He does not command us to heal them.

What does that have to do with the single person? you may ask. Some of the fiercest stings in single living come when people try to fix things themselves. Then if the hurting person fails to respond in a certain way, you either accuse him of having little faith or leave him for not responding.

Why not try a visit instead? Or have him or her over. That way God can do the inside restoring.

One night around your fire, even when things are not perfect at home, becomes a gold mine for the single who is alone all week. That leftover supper sitting at the back of your refrigerator tastes better to him than caviar does alone. Remember, he is more likely to be himself when you are. So if the house is a mess, don't fret. But only God can restore and heal.

Don't be disappointed if your friend fails to take quantum leaps toward maturity each time you pray. God draws each one close while He teaches. Often months drag by with one lesson barely caught. Don't give up. Remember, love accepts. And love hangs in. But it never fails.

Encourage the Person to Be Content in Christ

We could all spend a lifetime looking at both our sins and our hopes. But a few learn to look past both to Christ. This secret frees a person. When a broken person looks up, she finds wholeness. Now she is ready to bless others while quietly waiting on God to bless her.

The single parent is different from other parents in one respect. She looks to the rules for both father and mother and then adapts the family principles through the broken glass of one lens. But she is remarkably similar, too. She wants to see her children whole, and she needs guidance in times of difficulty. While she needs love desperately, if you feel sorry for her you'll never see her grow. But if you're willing to take the risk and befriend her, you'll find by revelation that *love never fails!*

Bible Study Suggestions

Proverbs 17:9,17; 27:6,10; John 15:13-15

Practical Applications

1. Who can you share deepest concerns with?

2. Have you left relationships pouting or angry? You may need to go back and ask forgiveness before restoration takes place.

3. When is it wise to take advice? When not?

4. List what you'd like in a close friend. Now ask God to help you be that to somebody. Watch the joy that flows from "being" a friend.

5. How do you feel you might get to know Christ as friend on a deeper level?

4

God Turns My Ashes into Gold

"I'm sorry about Matthew's swollen eye," Miss Clay told Doreen, his mother, after our church service. "He was led into a tree."

The grade two class had a lesson on walking by faith and not by sight. One child was told to close his eyes, take the hand of his partner, and walk around the church grounds. Things went well until Gordie, Matthew's partner passed the big oak tree cater-cornered to the church and forgot to steer Matthew. Matthew, with every confidence in his nine-year-old leader, veered off to his left and slammed headlong into the oak.

Miss Clay panicked. *What if the kids miss the whole point of today's class?* she wondered. But four years teaching grade two children provided her with that quick alternative plan. The lesson changed to: "Look to God, and never to mankind."

God turns our blunders around. Just like the teacher, He uses them for our good. But unless you give them over, you get stuck with defeat.

The choice is simple. Fall victim to your circumstances or choose to control them. If, for instance, you find yourself waiting for the mail each day in case something good might happen, watch out. Or if you head for a lottery line thinking a windfall might wipe out your emptiness, you'll fall victim. But, if you count on God's love to sweep away the blues, you trade your weakness for heaven's strength every time. And His love never depends on a person's good performance.

39

For years the real me hid behind walls of anger, unforgiveness, and regret. I worked hard for approval, but I never felt worthy to accept it.

Then, ten years into marriage, my husband found another woman and left. In one swoop I lost everything we had built, and my heart sank again. But God came at my lowest point. My brother and sister-in-law, Tom and Dolores, came by within the first few days of our break and told me how to place my life in the hands of Someone who'd never turn away: Jesus. I've never looked back!

When despair grips you, hold onto Jesus, and He'll guide you back into His joy. No matter what the problem, you can find courage.

Are you exhausted? Do you need a holiday but instead stare at an empty bankbook? Remember, nothing is too difficult for God. If you do a little planning, I have found that you can come up with just the right breakaway! But what if you have no money? There are still options! The challenge of planning a good holiday on very little was the beginning of an adventure for us.

"School's out, Mom. Let's do something crazy today!" Tan met me in the in the hall at 3:50 PM on the last day.

"We'll get the groceries later," I agreed, catching her enthusiasm."

We decided to stop and grab a few weiners and walk down to the park near the water. As we sat under the weeping willow and watched the sun go down, we stretched out on the warm rocks and dangled our feet. For a few minutes we sat there, content to be part of nature's orchestra. Rhythmic splashes cheered on two young gulls just overhead. Instead of looking at what was far beyond our abilities we would look for something closer to home, which fit us. This was a new day! Our itinerary was drawn up. We planned seven days that would take the tiredness out of our bones after a long term. The emphasis was fun!

Our first week went like this:

Day One: All the appointments for committee work or fall planning that ran into the summer were canceled. We simply explained that we were going on a holiday. People understood! Then we slept in on purpose. We breakfasted together on the patio. Then, after a brisk walk we drew up the plan. Duty first, I decided. So we washed clothes and put the house in order. Now we could enjoy our new freedom.

Day Two: Walking would be the main means of transportation whenever possible. We decided to save on gas and get into shape. If we had to go any distance, we took our bikes. To get the muscles working we walked over to the university grounds, took a tour, and then sat with the newspaper over coffee in the lounge. The bus trip home took us past streets we had never been on, and we talked to a few new people.

Day Three: Whatever added to a laugh in our home was welcomed. We listened to tapes from Lake Wobegon, spent time reminiscing about some of the silly things that happened during the year, and made up jokes. We laughed at ourselves, each other, and life in general. Then we put together the highlights of our year in an old album, using a few pictures we had and drawing the rest. We took turns writing the captions under the snapshots and added a few insights to fun times we had with friends.

Day Four: Our main library was the next stop. All those books and magazines that we had no time for . . . now smothered our attention! We brought lunch and spent the day. There were even distractions that were fun. Tan seemed to enjoy looking up titles by her favorite authors on the new computers. I listened to a little classical music. When we left with two armloads of reading material, we knew we'd be going all over the world *free* in the next few days!

Day Five: In our city the extensive museum just happens to be free. After discussing a few of the things we'd never really noticed on a dash through, we decided to stay and take in two films being shown. The manager must have known about our resolution to laugh; he chose a Laurel and Hardy and a ridiculous film about baby sea lions for the group.

Day Six: By day six we were tired. We'd hiked enough. So we planned a day at home. It was overcast, so we opened the windows and lit a cozy fire. Then we got our Christmas lists out. Things were getting expensive; we decided to have a crafts day and begin to make the gifts while we had time. I made some books by taking old pictures, stories, and cards, and adding my own writing to suit the family I'd be giving it to. We mimicked things they had done and drew cartoons to illustrate. Making gifts that would be appreciated by our closest friends gave us much pleasure.

Day Seven: After a good time of laughing, talking, and "catching up," we were ready to go again. An invitation to spend a day with friends on the ranch had come months earlier. We wrapped some weiners and buns in brown paper and set out at 5:00 A.M. for the two-hour drive. Just as the sun was peeking over the hills we passed a sidewalk cafe. I took a quick left, and we watched the sunrise over hot chocolate and toast. By 7:45 we were in the middle of a family of seven, four cats, three dogs, and 600 heifers. The dogs and the kids ran out to welcome us as we drove in the winding driveway. It felt like old home week. We slept over.

While the adults sat over iced tea on the patio, the kids ran off to do the chores. Then we all strolled to the lake for a swim. Around a crackling fire that night we sang some of the old hymns and a few folk tunes.

Near midnight the next day we rounded the curve for our own street. I asked Tanya how she enjoyed her holiday. "It's great, Mom," she said sleepily. "What's on for tomorrow?"

"The sky's the limit," I answered. "Why don't we just plan for the week again. This week we'll include window-shopping, a day at the park, and horseback riding. Who knows? We might meet some Egyptian camels!"

The secret was in our attitudes. It may be hard to get away. You probably have very little money after tuition, rent, food, and medical expenses. I received no alimony or monthly help, so I had to take on the whole load after losing everything.

There were no relatives to greet us at the other end. But don't let any of these hurdles steal good family fun, memories, and much needed leisuretime.

Once I jumped in and made the decision, it was easier. Don't be afraid to go alone. You will meet others who are alone also. I even tried to reach out to some of them. Once I saw God's protection and care, I found it a challenge to go places alone and give out to others.

On one of our walks we decided to stop at the pet store. Two recent arrivals caught our eye immediately. They were both sitting in identical cages near the entrance to the pet shop: two Congo-African grey parrots, with bright red-orange tails—the only contrast to their soft grey feathers. At first glance they could have been twins, alike in every way, but one.

With a sign reading "Angel" hung like a tilted halo over his head, the little fellow was full of fun. He made noises like corks popped from the bottle's neck, wolf whistled with delight every time a lady came by, and hopped around looking for ways to entertain every guest who came near.

The other, Kaptain, growled and hissed at each one who came near. After a few attempts to communicate and make friends, the crowds left his cage, drawn like magnets to Angel. I wondered if the young bird knew why all the people wanted to be around his brother and nobody stayed with him. The fact is, we are often like Kaptain, barring all the fun that attracts the people we need most around us to join in.

Interestingly, the sign over Kaptain read: "$500.00. I'm not very tame yet." Over Angel was written: "Hi, I'm Angel. I love people, but I'm not for sale."

When you laugh, you splash new colors on your surroundings. Even mistakes look different. Friends want to be around you.

But do you ever see yourself in Kaptain? Do you snarl at things you can't handle and hiss at your problems? Do your friends only hear stories of woe?

Why not have a little fun? Just watch what happens when you let go and let God.

It's a matter of priority. When you look at the day with all its responsibilties, when you have no family to call on and no partner, it looks staggering. So you tend to drop off all the laughing matters and add more time for the practical things. What a pity! The house always needs cleaning or the car washing. Hardly do I remember a night that I finished correcting English papers before I dropped into bed exhausted after midnight. Only to rise at 5:00 AM before the whole routine repeated itself.

A single parent has plenty to be grim about. Someone once said: "The trouble with life is that it is so daily." But we can overcome rather than be overcome! Remember the words of Jesus: "In this world you will have trouble. But take heart! I have overcome the world" (John 16:33).

Why not get into the Scriptures? Remind yourself of God's promise to take care of you, and chuck the worries. Choose a merry heart, the best medicine, and smile even in a sea of frowns.

Laughter is an important part of God's nature, and many times laughter is appropriate, even necessary. On the other hand, who can bear a sad heart and a broken spirit?

We've all heard the infectious giggles of children. Or remember that evening you sat around laughing with an old friend? The next funny incident is only as far away as the person who enjoys humor.

So take advantage of the little family happenings. You'll always wash away those blues and tie up anxieties when you laugh.

The joke may even be on you. We had someone looking in the kitchen window after dark one night. When our landlord found out, he was furious, saying: "Just pound on the ceiling, and I'll be down like a flash if it ever happens again."

A few months went by with no incident. Then one night we finished a good game of Scrabble at about 11:00 PM, and Tanya was in a silly mood. She stood under a low beam in the hallway of our basement suite and yelled: "Look, there's only a few inches left. Then she impulsively leaped into the air to measure her free distance and rammed her head into the beam.

We both thought we heard our landlord jump up, and we were sure he'd be down to club the intruder. So Tanya grabbed the telephone and said: "Hi, Ralph, I just banged my head."

"Oh, you sure are getting tall. Is it all right now?" the surprised voice on the other end of the phone replied.

The next day our landlord's daughter told us he was sound asleep when the phone rang. At the breakfast table he announced: "Tanya phoned me at 11:00 last night to tell me she bumped her head!"

One little incident, but we laughed till we split. Every time we thought of it for weeks we laughed.

Bible Study Suggestions

John 2:1-11; Matthew 11:25; 26:27; John 11:41; David: 1 Chronicles 25:1-3; 2 Chronicles 5:12-13; Daniel 2:23; Jonah 2:9; Simeon: Luke 2:28; Anna: Luke 2:38; Paul: Acts 28:15.

Practical Applications

1. Show how Jesus set an example of thankfulness. Matthew 11:25; 26:27; John 11:41

2. How was each of the following thankful, and for what?

a. David: 1 Chronicles 25:1-3

b. Levites: 2 Chronicles 5:12-13

c. Daniel 2:23

d. Jonah 2:9

e. Simeon: Luke 2:28

f. Anna: Luke 2:38

g. (Paul)-Acts 28:15

3. How did Jesus relate fun with the truths of the Scriptures?
4. List three ways you and your children have fun.
5. Can you think of any way to relate these fun times with the principles of God's kingdom.

5
Let God Love You

While we know in theory that God's love is enough to answer the deepest needs of the heart, we often miss its touch when we need it most. Who can say with conviction, "His love has never failed me"?

A confused 14-year-old girl sat in my English class blotting the tears with her free hand while she copied notes on how Hamlet outwitted Claudius. "It reminds me of my father," she confessed after class when I stopped her on the way out. "It's not just my mom he hates, it's me too."

Trying to comfort her I replied, "I'm sure he really loves you deep down." (I lied!)

Teri gulped, "Nobody in my house loves anybody, and I don't care."

As she grabbed her purse off the edge of her chair and ran to her science class, I prayed, "Lord, reveal Your bigger love to Teri today. Put Your big arms around her in a real way."

Few would deny that God's intimate love is always available to us. Yet we miss its application when we only look in the usual places and ignore the unusual. I was touched by His love a few weeks ago for instance by a tug and a handful of wild flowers.

Earlier that evening, as I maneuvered my car through the storm to the worship service, there was an anticipation in my spirit. A group of well-known Israeli musicians were to be in the evening service.

"Get there early if you want a seat," Pastor Johnson had warned that morning. "We're expecting a big crowd!"

I thought of the memorable time we had when they came two years ago. Four churches packed our sanctuary to join us for the event. The orchestra strings danced while modern keyboards holding five, distinct, grand piano tunes filled the stadium; and three violins swelled our worship into the heavens. We sang the praises of the Lord until late that night while couples clad in Israel's bright national costumes performed before the Lord in concert.

Within the music I remembered sensing the distinct cry of the Lord to come into His presence lifting holy hands.

"Lord, they brought Your love to us before!" I reminded Him through the humming wipers as I approached the church. "You were so high and lifted up in our worship that night. We touched Your very beauty and holiness."

The place was packed. An usher led me to one wedge in the third row as the band opened with an upbeat Israeli chorus, and I slipped my coat over the back of the bench. As I turned I caught a glimpse of the congregation. From the grim expressions of some to the radiant smiles of a few, I had an overwhelming sense of my own need for His love.

Give us a new revelation of Your love tonight, I prayed, while the worship peaked. Just then a gentle tug on my skirt drew my attention from our celebrities, and I glanced down in its direction.

There stood five-year-old Geoffrey with a little bouquet of freshly cut daisies in his hand. "Do you like these?" he whispered, loud enough I was sure for the people around us to hear. It wasn't even the flowers clasped in Geoffrey's hand, but it was the expression of Christ in this young boy's face that moved me to stop singing and bend down to smell his flowers.

Sounds of worship echoed in the sanctuary all around us, but my thoughts were far removed from the words now. Geoffrey lifted up his treasured bouquet and whispered, "They're for you!"

Then he placed them gently into my hand and headed back

across the aisle as quietly as he had come to sit with his brother. He glanced back a final exchange and turned to face the singers.

Still holding my gift I looked around at the faces of the worshipers. By the raised hands and closed eyes I knew that the people around me were standing in God's presence and adoring Him. But I wondered if they could each feel His tangible love that Geoffrey brought to me.

Jesus used a young boy who gave his lunch so that a hungry crowd would be fed. Now a child brought me another expression of Christ's love, and it came in the form of a few wilted daisies. Christ's response to my prayer in worship: He sent His love through a small child.

I would have looked for Him in the band or tried to follow the words of the songs for my expression of His love. But Geoffrey showed me where it was that night.

I vowed, "Lord, I will not restrict Your love again. I will be watching for Your presence in the unusual places."

It might be that He wants to surprise you and send His extravagant love to you in some unsuspecting way as He did to me that night through Geoffrey's daisies.

So often I could have gone on with more courage if I had felt God's love. Many times He was trying to show love to me and I failed to recognize His touch.

Sometimes pride got in the way. A dear young pastor friend told me about God's dealings in his life to remove pride. Jeff had one secret dream: to preach mainly so he could have his name in the newspaper. The day finally came. Jeff's pastor asked him to speak on Sunday night the next week. All week Jeff felt the excitement of seeing his name. First thing Saturday morning he flung the paper open, and there they were—the magic words, right under his senior pastor's name.

But before he could go to the service, Jeff had and emergency call where he worked as ambulance driver. As the middle-aged woman was lifted onto the stretcher she experienced great abdominal discomfort and indicated she was going to be sick. They grabbed the newspaper just in time and flipped at random to Jim's name. Bull's-eye! The lady hit dead on.

"And that," God spoke to Jim's heart, "is what pride brings."

While Jim laughed about this story, I saw very little pride in his life. How convinced I was of the pride that sat in my own life still undealt with. When we boast, we have only Christ, who saved us from the pit of destruction and who delivers us daily to brag about. But He is more than enough!

When I know my position in God, I can say with the Shulamite, "I am the rose of Sharon, and the lily of the valleys" (Song of Sol. 2:1, KJV). She knew she belonged to her beloved, and he was hers. That is enough to carry anyone through the winters and safely into spring.

Love has failed every single parent at least once and, therefore, left some mark. There is often a pain of separation from those we still care deeply about. And the Lord does not ask us to deny our feelings here.

Dietrich Bonhoeffer made four observations about separation from those we love, which I often found comfort in:

First: Nothing can make up for the absence of someone we love, and it would be wrong to try to find a substitute; we must simply hold out and see it through. That sounds very hard at first, but at the same time it is a great consolation, for the gap as long as it remains unfilled, preserves the bonds between us. It is nonsense to say that God fills the gap; he doesn't fill it, but on the contrary, he keeps it empty and so helps us to keep alive our former communication with each other, even at the cost of pain.

Second: The dearer and richer our memories, the more difficult the separation. But gratitude changes the pangs of memory into a tranquil joy. The beauties of the past are born, not as a thorn in the flesh, but as a precious gift in themselves. We must take care not to wallow in our memories or hand ourselves over to them, just as we do not gaze all the time at a valuable present, but only at special times, and apart from these keep it simply as a hidden treasure that is ours for certain. In this way the past gives us lasting joy and strength.

Third: Times of separation are not a total loss or unprofitable for our companionship, or at any rate they need not be so. In spite of all the difficulties that they bring, they can be the means of strengthening fellowship quite remarkably.

Fourth: I've learned here especially that the facts can always be mastered, and that difficulties are magnified out of all proportion simply by fear and anxiety. From the moment we wake until we fall asleep we must commend other people wholly and unreservedly to God and leave them in his hands, and transform our anxiety for them into prayers on their behalf: With sorrow and grief . . . God will not be distracted.[1]

When I came to the place where I invited Christ to be my all in all, I received more confidence in His love. Unlike my own expressions of love, I often discovered the Lord's love is down to earth, concrete, and often comes through others when I least expect it. It is unconditional, never waiting for a person to deserve it. But it is always given on God's terms!

Letting God love me, for instance, meant I had to receive His discipline. The Lord tells us: "Those whom I love I rebuke and discipline" (Rev. 3:19).

The purpose of God's love is to transform us into His own image. As our Heavenly Father, how much more He loves us than our earthly fathers. When we let His love mold our behavior, we find peace. Larry Christenson showed this strong bond between love and discipline in the natural child's relationship with his father:

Every parent has had the experience of watching a child grow more and more disobedient until the exasperated parent finally bursts out, "You're just asking for a spanking!" If only the parent realized how literally true that is, it would not have to tune up to the point of exasperation. The child's understanding is not mature. He cannot articulate the reason for his discontent, for he does not have an intellectual grasp of it. But his spirit, nevertheless has a clear intuitive grasp of the basic issue. His discontent is related to disobedience. . . . The child is asking for a spanking in the only way he knows how. Not many children will grasp this intellectually, like the seven year old who said to his father after a sound trouncing: "Thank you, Daddy. That did me good!" But every child will know a deep contentment of spirit when he is helped to walk in the ways of obedience. For this is the focus and expression of his relationship with Jesus.[2]

Rejection, the thing that often separates the single parent from experiencing God's love, can actually be a stepping-stone to receiving that love. When this painful condition grips you, you are faced with a choice. You can use it positively or flee behind a wall until it destroys. I discovered rejection can be an ingredient for love, if I encounter His presence whenever I feel its sting.

Even if rejection stalks like a thief in the night, you do not need to be its helpless victim. The key is to respond, not react. The Lord will become your "rejection Bearer" if we let Him. He understood this trial better than anyone:

> He was despised and rejected by men,
> a man of sorrows, and familiar with suffering.
> Like one from whom men hide their faces
> he was despised, and we esteemed him not
> (Isa. 53:3).

Rejection can be the instrument that flings one into the Lord's arms. For the single parent there is much comfort in the knowledge that God loves unconditionally. Meditating on the Scriptures helps us remember that the Lord will never leave us or forsake us. No matter who left in the past or who we rejected, He promised to never turn His back on us. That truth will bring strength and healing to a person stung by rejection.

Because God desires all our devotion, He sometimes allows people we trust most to desert us for a time. For me this was an experience I met after I accepted the Lord and joined a church. God wanted to teach me a higher dependency. He wanted to become my All in all!

The Lord wants our full surrender, our full attention. He wants freedom to reign in His fullness within our hearts. Just as He carried the Shulamite out of the wilderness, to leave behind her life of wanderlust, He will carry each one out (Song of Sol. 3:6). When Christ brings us out, it is with healing in His wings. We too will be perfumed with the myrrh of His indwelling cross and the sweet odor of frankincense which speaks of the pure frangrance of the cross's fruits.

We acquire new strength when He takes us through. Our desires are soon set in His love alone, and trust in His keeping power takes root. Once we know that experimentally, we hold onto a truth for comfort in dry times.

If you look to God alone for appreciation and comfort, you receive love based on the finished work of the cross. If you look inward for self-appreciation or depend on others to meet the need for approval, it will fail at the most critical times.

My tendency was to work hard for love. When others did not respond, I fell into self-condemnation. Of course, the ones on whom I placed expectations did not understand. God allowed every work to fail so He could show me unconditional, free love.

God's love does not flee or change by our whims. It is always there to see you through. He loves you enough to fashion you into His own image. And He is gentle and patient. You may not always feel loved. But hang in, and you'll question love less and less.

The continual flow of God's love requires that we give it out to others, drawing deep from its source in God. Not until I found myself alone in life did I begin to understand the loneliness of shut-ins and widows left alone. As I reached out, God seemed to pour much more love back into my life in extravagant ways. I noticed when I got down in the dumps that I was not reaching out and that the magic flow seemed to vanish.

When you are secure in God's love, you relate better to those around you. Then you are ready to take an active part in the body: His extended family. Conversly, when you will not allow God's love to flow into your life, you are like the condemned building, ready to be destroyed. You drain strength from others but have none to pour back.

Have you ever had the joy of knowing a person who basks in God's love? Just being with that person warms your heart. My dear friend, Brenda, who suffers with a rare disease is one of these. Even though she is dying and is only in her twenties, she sings of His love and goodness constantly. Brenda's words have often echoed the thoughts of Hannah Hurnard, from *Mountain of Spices*.

> Do not fear the cutting knife,
>   Do not shrink in pain,
> Let the red drops of thy life
>   Fall like bleeding rain.
> That which thee to death dost give,
> Is the seed which yet shall live.
>
> Do not fear the winter's breath,
>   Let the seed drop to the earth,
> Everything laid down to death
>   Waits a resurrection birth.
> Let the flower drop; on the thorn
> Fairer glories shall be born.
>
> Do not let self-pity bleed
>   Bitterness, nor fierce regret.
> These are worms which kill the seed,
>   And sad misery beget.
> With a willing heart let go,
> God will richer gifts bestow.
>
> Learn the lesson, fast or slow,
>   This is heaven's law,
> We must let the old things go,
>   To make room for more.

We shall reap in some glad way,
fairer joys than lost today.[3]

We all sing, "Jesus loves me! this I know." But do we *know* with certainty? I used to think 1 Corinthians 13, that famous love chapter, was about my love for you. Not so. It's about God's love for you and me. Once I saw that and accepted God's perfect love, I found myself in a better place to love you. You might say I had some love to give now.

Tanya discovered the power of love in her attempt to win over a cantankerous cockatiel. James was probably an escapee from a local bird sanctuary. It was reported vandalized about the time he was found in a tree and adopted. James' first family tried to house him with another cockatiel and four parakeets, but he proved too set in his ways for them. Then a second family took him in, but poor old James didn't fare much better with them. He took to their little female cockatiel immediately though. All seemed well until her husky mate let James know with a bite to the neck what the price of further intrusion would be. Poor James. He huddled miserably in the corner of the aviary and sulked for three days. He refused to eat or come out. This was too much for his second family, so Tanya was presented with her first bird.

James snapped at her and hissed like a cat whenever anybody came near. He often drew blood, and when Tan asked a bird trainer what she could do, the advice was: "Wear protective gloves. An older bird who bites that hard will never change."

Tanya and I talked about how God's love changed us. And Tanya decided that love could win her renegade bird over too. So every time James bit her, Tanya calmly blew on his beak. But she refused to wear gloves or draw love away. Tanya even tried to hide the gashes on her hands from me because I had less faith in love's power to win James.

By the end of the second month we noticed James's affection for Tanya. He would sing, wolf whistle, and hop up and down on his bar when she opened the door after school. Then, when Tanya walked away from James, he tilted his little head to the side in a hilarious pose. He'd often peek around the corner, watching her until she was out of sight.

Finally one day, James flew out of the cage onto Tanya's shoulder while she brushed her hair in the mirror. Now he travels everywhere with her. When she practices her guitar, he patiently sits on a nearby perch and waits. Then he flies back to her finger. I can't join in their musical conversations. Only they know the interpretation. But I sense with each note that theirs is a language of love, friendship, and understanding.

James wolf whistles often for Tanya. But he acts rather aggressive with me when I go in to wake her up in the morning. It seems they have an arrangement worked out—James holds the watch while Tanya grabs a little extra shut-eye.

Love tamed one seemingly hopeless little bird. He rarely bites now. The Bible tells us that love never fails, and I like to think that's God's kind of love. (See 1 Cor. 13.)

I missed His love when I needed it most. But I've learned a few keys to help me accept His unconditional love that might help you:

1. Accept the fact that God loves you for what He did, not for what you can do for Him. Calvary settled the height of God's love that I would receive. It is perfect. Nothing will change the amount of love God has for every person.

2. Look for evidence of God's love in every trial you run into. Put away the idea that God is punishing you when hardships come. Amazing things happen when we see our problems through His eyes.

3. Thank God for His love often. This acknowledges love and brings joy into our lives in a new way.

4. Pass love onto others. As we give love, it bounces back one-hundredfold. But love that is hoarded dries up before it has much effect on the owner. God's love increases as we give it away.

5. Don't try and earn God's love. No striving will make it grow. But the good news is, you get it free.

6. Drop your negative thoughts about any lack of love you received from others. Some people miss God's love because they still gripe about no love in their youth. Others demand love from others and refuse to see that God's love is sufficient. When persons let go of complaints, they are open to receive.

7. Forgive anybody who withheld love in anyway. Release them with your will and ask God to fill that place with His love.

8. Never accept self-pity. It will rob you from receiving God's love faster than any other emotion.

9. Ask God to reveal His love to you in new ways, and then expect it. Those who ask, receive. But we need to ask, believing.

10. Remember in every situation in which you find yourself: *love never fails.*

Bible Study Suggestions

Song of Solomon 2—3.

Practical Applications

1. Who does the Shulamite represent?

2. Why can she call herself the rose of Sharon, the lily of the valleys?

3. What did she do to earn love?

4. What does verse 6 mean?

5. What does her lover tell her about the winter's hardships?

6. What are the little foxes?

7. What condition is she in when her lover carries her out of the wilderness?

8. Find a set time each day that suits your schedule to spend with the Lord. Start with 15 minutes and gradually add minutes until you are spending at least one hour a day in prayer and Bible reading.

Notes

1. *Letters and papers from Prison* (New York: The Macmillan Co., ©
1953, 1967, 1971 by SCN Press, Ltd.), 176-177
   2. *The Christian Family* (Minneapolis: Bethany House, 1970).
   3. (Wheaton: Tyndale House, 1975).

6
The Joy of Extended Family

Brother V. A. Joseph, a missionary in South India, took home a few dirty orphans in 1975. He found the children wandering around the streets with the oxcarts and beggars in India's most primitive villages. Word soon got around that Joseph cared. And kids just kept coming. One morning the family woke to an infant's cries. There on the front step was a newborn baby boy, shivering in the rain.

Today, Joseph has 33 children and hopes to take in more. "They are all family," he told me. A friend who spent several months helping the missionary shared how: "The kids love Joseph. They all call him Daddy."

Are you wandering alone in a tough place? God, your Father, cares about you more than anybody else can. A poster on my kitchen door shows two men's hands stretched heavenward. Below, it reads: "There is an insatiable hunger within each of us that God alone can satisfy." While it's true that God meets the deepest longings of your heart, no one can make it alone. You need close, vulnerable ties with others. And those around you, need you.

Family was the first social structure God produced. He saw the need for us to have companionship. Children were meant to be the fruit of their parent's relationship.

So why do the experts tell us one in three teens thinks about suicide? Why are struggling families among today's street people? Why do we have child abuse, drug abuse, divorce, spouse abuse, teenage rebellion, pornography, and abortion at rates we've never seen before? Why so many single parents?

The fact is: God made us dependent, but we too often opt for independance. Our disobedience to God's laws brings its own consequences. But God will never turn His back on you. There is a vital place for you in His family. He will direct you to that place if you'll let Him.

Three nights ago, one of Tanya's friends from school accepted the Lord as her Savior in a glorious time of sharing around our kitchen table. Now 16-year-old Sherrie wants to join us for church. We told her about our church family and how they'd love her. As we sipped coffee that first night together, Sherrie had a tough time seeing how God's family—the body of Christ—could be related to her.

For 13 years my church has also been family. Not that it's been all easy. Just the opposite. Did you ever wonder why you have a hard time loving someone? We let one another down consistently. But through it all we learn to look for those precious treasures in earthern vessels: God's kids. And I wouldn't trade them for a million dollars. Parents, grandparents, brothers, sisters, and cousins—all sent by God. Tanya is loved and cared for in this family in practical ways. So if I have to travel, I have a place to leave her. And Tanya gets invited overnight. Even the kids forged bonds that went beyond friendships.

Things were just the opposite for Sherrie. Her parents were usually drunk. Her mother went to court last week to answer fraud charges and could be jailed. Sherrie has never met her grandparents or cousins. Two brothers and one sister are married and live in another city.

Sherrie especially liked to join us for "family" dinners. Whenever we'd invite groups over, she was right there. But she rarely spoke up. One day I caught her just staring as each one of the kids told cat stories around the kitchen table. We always included Sherrie when we could. And, gradually, Sherrie told her own sto-

ries until you couldn't keep up with her. This was the very first
family who just loved her for being herself. Sherrie started baby-
sitting and then would ask to sleep over to avoid parties at home.

Our extended family always had room for one more. That's what
distinguishes God's family from other groups. There is no exclusive
membership. Nobody is ever shut out when Christ is at the center.
Jesus drew crowds because everyone saw His love for them personally. He was moved in compassion to feed, heal, and teach.

The plain truth is: we all need Sherrie as much as she needs us.
I used to think I could make it alone. Not so. We need each other,
and not one of us is excluded in God's economy. Why fear rejection
when God loves you? Why fear exposure?

Remember what God promised:

Fear not, for I have redeemed you;
I have called you by your name; you are mine.
When you pass through the waters,
    I will be with you;
and when you pass through the rivers,
    they will not sweep over you.
When you walk through the fire, you will not be burned;
    The flames will not set you ablaze.
For I am the Lord, your God (Isa. 43:1-3).

Are you alone through separation or divorce? Have you lost
somebody you loved? Remember one thing. You will not be destroyed by this hurt. God will take you through it. Hold His hand.
He won't ever let go. Then take your place in His family.

Outside the body of Christ there are no binding relationships
that last. When the storms come, the sand houses tumble. Only
Christ, the Rock can bind. Only God is Love! And it is really His
love we share. That is why Sherrie was so welcomed into God's
family and warmed by it.

Today's church is just at the tip of the iceberg in reaching the
potential God intends for extended family. Some say the pendulum

swung too far in the sixties. Some communes separated young couples who chose to live together and support one another. Many of these failed to grasp the freedom and maturity that God intended for each one of us. Some caught themselves in traps of serving a leader instead of serving God. Others were forced to submit to human beings rather than to God. But most were looking for a method of binding members together with a common bond. When these groups forgot to look to their Head Christ, they plummeted. A few survived though.

Home fellowships often serve to bind together an extended family in today's churches. They meet every few days, often with events scheduled in between. It was at a home cell group that my extended family first took shape. God sent just the right people, even though many would not have been the ones I would have chosen. They were His choice, and today I can see why.

One lady in her early eighties, Elena, was everybody's grandma. We found any excuse to get together just to have her around. She was the kind of person who grew old in her body but kept all the vigor of the youngest among the family when it came to everyday life. Like the time we all went camping, and Elena fell in the lake trying to tug a lily pad out of the reeds. She wanted a centerpiece for our picnic table! Elena's a lot like the Skin Horse: she's real.

When the Velveteen Rabbit asked the Skin Horse, "What is *real?* Does it mean having things that buzz inside you and a stick-out handle?" The Skin Horse tried to show him the ability that only an older person has to be real. He explained why Elena, the oldest one in our fellowship, won our love:

> "It doesn't happen all at once," Said the Skin Horse. "You become. It takes a long time. That's why it doesn't often happen to people who break easily, or have sharp edges, or have to be carefully kept. Generally, by the time you are real, most of your hair has been loved off, and your eyes drop out and you get loose in the joints and very shabby. But these things don't matter at all because once you are Real you can't be ugly, except to people who don't understand."[1]

It seems foreign at first. We shrink from reaching out to anybody new. The Lord taught me the value of extended family bit by bit. Each time I obeyed and opened my arms to share His love to another person, God increased His love back to me.

One afternoon I took a stroll along the ocean near my home where I learned my first lesson. I was lost in my own thoughts until I stumbled upon a middle-aged lady with her head down as if counting the pebbles.

The still small voice in my heart urged me to go over and meet this lady. I argued that I didn't know her, and I probably couldn't help her anyway. But the Lord persisted, until I walked over.

The Holy Spirit was teaching me to appreciate God's children more. The woman explained how she found out a few hours before that she had a very serious cancer. By becoming her sister and sharing God's love with her, I was able to support and comfort her. Not long after the operation, Mardi gave her heart to the Lord and serves among the elderly in hospitals today. All because family surrounded her when she was alone in trouble, one woman came through cancer rejoicing in God's goodness.

But what about those days when everything goes wrong? The kids are fighting, and you have to change your tire before you back the car out of the driveway. These days especially, you'll be glad to have a family in place. Those who change churches every few months miss the joy of extended family. Or if you attend a big congregation and don't get involved in smaller groups, others won't get the chance to know you. Forming a strong family takes time. Superficial relationships are born in a moment and grow as fast as the mushroom through a rainy night. Some are afraid to put roots down into a lasting bond and wait. They run into times of difficulty. But for those who do linger, their lives will be as strong in storms as the life within an oak tree. It, too, took time and watering.

Extended families give you a place to take off masks, to be real, like the skin horse. For me there were other benefits. Just dropping by another family for coffee, or having people call in on us was a treat. And because they are "family," you have the freedom to say, "Not today; thanks."

Tanya grew up with other Christian kids in close relationships. She baby-sat with some, played chess with others, and even battled with a few. But they cared more than "neighborhood" gangs. They listened to one another as teens. When there were problems, I often heard Tanya pray for them or comfort them.

When Tanya is ready to leave my home, she will have a mesh of homes to come back to. Only after years in the church did I see the deep bonds. But they were forming all the time. As your children date and marry, they will carry a treasury of strong family relationships into one another's lives. With God's love, their generation can fill some of the gaps blown into families in ours.

Walls come down in a family. Even walls that build up in a church. Watch where persons build their strongest defense, and you'll see where they're most vulnerable. We try to shield ourselves most in vulnerable areas. We're afraid if we expose who we really are, we'll be rejected.

Did you ever long to unmask a group, so you too could take your mask off? I did. Why not try it first in a group you come to love and trust because they belong to God? You will not find perfect circles, but once I could become real with others, I found myself wanting to love again. Loneliness and despair flee in the wake of strong family ties.

Admit your own weakness, and you'll find others trust you more. The opposite to being real is to play games. You put on a front, pretend you're something you're not. You worry, *What if somebody finds me out?* Your own heart condemns you.

Others see only the guards you hide behind, never the real you. Your perfect hairdo and well-groomed look might fool a few. But those who know you will eventually turn away. What a lonely place that pretense is. When I quit teaching to write full-time, I tried to hide how poor we were. I didn't want my church to think I was a parasite. So I hid how things really were. A deacon phoned one time to ask if we had food. "We're doing fine," I lied. So we got none.

I once read a sign that put it well: If You're Too Proud (or Too Afraid) to Admit You Are Hurting, Don't Be Surprised if Nobody Seems to Care.

Jean Vanier met a mentally handicapped man in France and invited the man to share his life. He found the thick walls around his heart were torn down as they worked together. One gift the mentally handicapped can teach us is how to be real. Those who are, are content. Vanier went on from that encounter to lay down his life to bring communities (mostly mentally handicapped) together where people were allowed to be whoever they were. He discovered that we all have much poverty as well as many gifts. By admitting our poverty and developing our gifts, Christ is glorified, and we are happy.

Bible Study Suggestions

2 Samuel 19:24-30

Practical Applications

1. Why did Mephibosheth go down to meet David as the king returned from exile.

2. Notice how the boy was dressed. What did this show?

3. How does this relationship of Jonathan's son and David show its depth?

4. Name one close relationship you feel the Lord is encouraging in your life.

5. Ask the Lord to guide you in deciding three specific ways you might help or encourage this person.

6. In what ways are you willing to allow this person to have input into your life?

7. Do you know anybody who is without anybody to love? What could you do to make a difference?

Notes

1. Margery Williams, *The Velveteen Rabbit.*

7
See Self-Pity Flee

When Millicent Fenwick said: "Never feel self-pity, the most destructive emotion there is," he spoke from personal experience. "How awful to be caught up in the squirrel cage of self," he warned. He was right.

Self-pity robbed me of most of the freedom and joy that would have carried me through some tough places until I saw its grip and struck back. Then I turned around to see a better way.

"Why did You ask me to walk alone, Father?" I often asked. Then when no apparent answer came, I felt mighty sorry for myself. One day I tried to launch into a chapter for a textbook I was writing. After what seemed like an afternoon, I realized I could no longer meet my deadline on a questionnaire I was to add to the book. For hours I argued with my mind about my plight. Finally, bent over my desk with my head in my hands I said, "Please take my grieving over what happened away, Lord." And He did. I worked all night to make up for wasted time and caught the next day's mail with my additions.

When I tried the old standby: "Reach out to others," it just felt worse. I could not shake the crippling despair by that formula. As a matter-of-fact I wonder about the effectiveness of ever reaching out to others with this motive. Not much love or compassion triggers service that is done for selfish ends. I found I sank right back into the trap again as soon as I was alone.

The first step for me was: *recognize* self-pity for what it is and sweep it out with repentance. Not that it doesn't come back when you let down your defenses. Watch for the signs though. Usually it accompanied preoccupation with my circumstances. I remember one morning clearing my desk off to organize a new writing project. I was genuinely excited about this article. It had a sure home in a good publishing company.

Thoughts of the perfect lead raced for my attention until I saw the whole story ticker tape with clarity across my mind. Then I picked up a hurtful letter that had found its way to the bottom of papers on the desk and skimmed it through. I sat down and reread the punch line: "So we have decided it is not God's will to include you anymore in our trips."

It was the "not God's will" that was the stinger! These retreats to the lake came every summer with a group of Christians I grew to love. Even though I was alone, I seemed to fit in fine. But the others were in couples, and a few felt that God had another plan for their direction in the retreats. Somehow the reason didn't matter. "Unwanted," "exclusive," "we don't need you" flashed like neon lights driving out all my creative story ideas. *How could they tell me God was in it?* I kept asking, not to anyone in particular.

A still small Voice nudged me to stash the letter and get into the Word of God, but I ignored it. *They don't understand how much those retreats and the fellowship meant,* I argued with the written words in my hand. *How can they accuse God of wanting this? How can they ignore all He says in His Word about love and blame Him for their cold hearts.*

Suddenly, I could feel my emotional ship sinking fast, and part of me longed to get off before it hit the bottom again. But feelings were running too deep now. I had allowed my heart to gaze on the situation like David allowed his eyes to gaze on Bathsheba just before committing adultery.

In pain I sifted through some broken promises the group made to me as we vulnerably sat in God's presence the previous year. "We'll have many retreats like this," Jake had said. In my judgment of the group I saw coldness in their hearts where I had once enjoyed God's soft care.

My morning wasted, I tried every activity I could think of to distract my mind from what I thought was the cruel truth chasing me with jaws of steel. My own heart was living up to its reputation:

> The heart is deceitful above all things
> and beyond cure.
> who can understand it?
>
> (Jer. 17:9).

Then I saw it! Whenever I look into my heart for understanding, the best I come up with is *self.* And the flesh is at enmity with the things of God. That's why the pain. That's why I sank so badly everytime I looked at hurtful things with my own reason.

After I forgave the group in my heart and asked God's forgiveness for judging them, I got on with my project. The group never did change their decision, but it was no longer destroying my peace. I acknowledged God's love that sent Him to Calvary to die so I could enter into His presence. I remembered that my freedom came from *trusting* Him to work out the details of my life. The group's plans which no longer included me faded to the background in light of the warmth of His presence to my heart when I lifted it up in praise.

You might say, "Yes, but my hurt is worse than just being crossed off somebody's list for a holiday." Probably it is. But the same principles worked for me in tougher situations once I found them. The fact is: the single person is especially vulnerable to self-pity because he is alone when a partner would have helped him through things and shared the burden.

The person who applies God's principles to tough situations will not only find personal victory in the thing but will point the way out of pain to others:

Every day out of the dark night of suffering, shine forth uncon-
querable souls. With lights so vivid they brighten the way for others[1]

Redbook printed a moving story, in February, 1987, about Sia-
mese twins. The parents, Peter and Marlene Cody, had to decide
which way to go. Ruth and Verena, three and one-half years old,
may only live for 10 years. Joined hearts told the doctors any
operation to separate the girls would kill one and give only a 10
percent chance of life to the other. The couple already had another
child to consider.

Peter and Marlene both remembered the temptation toward
self-pity. But they decided to take the other route and bring their
babies home. These twins brought more love into the family than
they had ever known. Joy filled their hearts as the girls learned to
walk, moving sideways like little crabs until the stronger one dart-
ed on impulse to a new interest.

Alterations were made to every aspect of the home as others
rallied around the courageous couple to support them. Two dresses
buttoned up at the sides fit the girls comfortably, and the church
treated them like any other children.

Brutus saw self-pity's potential destruction through William
Shakespeare's pen when he proclaimed:

> There is a tide in the affairs of men
> Which taken at the flood leads on to fortune;
> Omitted, all the voyage of their life
> Is bound in shallows and in miseries.
> On such a full sea are we now afloat,
> And we must take the current when it serves,
> Or lose our ventures.[2]

Our current is the Holy's Spirit's breath and life. Our means of
taking it is faith! A person's feelings have nothing to do with the
determination to go God's way. As a matter of fact, they will often
point one in the wrong way. A person can only take hold of God
by understanding this. You don't have to deny your feelings. Just

don't follow them. Instead go God's way, and negative feelings will eventually turn and follow the path of grace. More and more a person's human emotions come into line when they have been subjected to the higher way: God's path.

Not that self-pity won't keep knocking. The devil knows just how to render us helpless. So it makes sense to suppose that he will try to woo us into his trap of misery.

The famous author and psychologist William James said:

> The attitude of unhappiness is not only painful, it is also mean and ugly.
>
> What can be more base and unworthy than the pining, puling, mumping mood, no matter by what outward ills it may have been endangered?
>
> What is more injurious to others?
>
> What less helpful as a way out of difficulty?
>
> It but fastens and perpetuates the trouble which occasioned it, and increases the total evil of the situation.

My early morning time with God has been my greatest weapon. He sees ahead into the day and pours enough strength to overcome every evil when He meets a yielded heart.

What one decides in that early morning meeting with the Lord will dictate how the tough places later in any day will be conquered. Some cooperation on our part helps:

> Whoever would love life
> and see good days
> must keep his tongue from evil
> and his lips from deceitful speech.
> He must turn from evil and do good;
> he must seek peace and pursue it.
> For the eyes of the Lord are on the righteous
> and his ears are attentive to their prayer,
> but the face of the Lord is against those who do evil
>
> (1 Pet. 3:10-12).

There comes a point in a person's maturity when he can detect

self-pity before it takes root. Then prayer is God's weapon for us
to withstand further attack. William Barclay said:

> Prayer is not flight; prayer is power. Prayer does not deliver a
> man from some terrible situation; prayer enables a man to face and
> to master the situation.

When prayer replaces self-pity, the ship steers through every
storm. Even though you may not always feel God's presence, faith
will take the helm and steer you through. George MacDonald
found that God withdrew His presence from his consciousness at
times when he grappled with the why and came up with:

> He wants to make us in His own image, choosing the good,
> refusing the evil. How should He affect this if He were always
> moving us from within, as He does at divine intervals, towards the
> beauty of holiness? In other words, God withdraws in order to give
> us the freedom of choosing anew whether we will pursue Him above
> all else.
>
> What can a person do when he finds his prayers bouncing back
> from the ceiling? . . . Fold the arms of your faith and wait in
> quietness until the light goes up in your darkness. Fold the arms of
> your faith, I say, but not of your action. Think of something you
> ought to do, and go do it. Heed not your feelings. Do your work.

When I was under fire from some critic who didn't like the way
I brought Tanya up or didn't think I was sending her to the right
school, I often forgot all of this. I ran like Elijah did from the
wicked Queen Jezebel. Just like him, I cried out in self-pity expecting the Lord to hear my complaints.

It was as I meditated on who Christ said I was that I began to
exercise my authority as His child. I saw that after salvation I
became His child in a very real sense. I was a joint heir with Christ.
Through the months, I gradually began to understand that a Christian, as child of a King, has authority from the Heavenly Father
in every situation.

The price was paid at the Cross! All I have to do is choose

Christ's way and then take His grace to walk in it. When I succumb to self-pity, I ignore my birthrights as a Christian. When I recognize who I am by the blood of Christ, I gain strength just from the comfort of being His child through every test He allows. I run more quickly to tell Him I need His help and that I want to choose His way, not mine.

I've often seen a great blessing from the Lord come into my lives just after I refused self-pity and stood up as a thankful child. One night I consciously decided to lift my heart and praise even though it hurt to do so. Later that night I was given the privilege of leading two fellow teachers into a salvation experience. They are now deacons in the church.

There are still times when I go to a prayer warrior friend to ask for prayer when I slip and let the monster in. But by recognizing it and seeing the joy of being free, I am never victimized like I was when I didn't understand my weapons for warfare.

Bible Study Suggestions

1 Kings 19:13-14; Job 30:25-31

Practical Applications

Self-pity is not a new emotion. It worked destruction in a few Bible character's lives, and will try in yours.

1. What were the reasons Elijah felt sorry for himself?

2. Why did Job feel self-pity?

3. What are some of the reasons a single person falls into self-pity?

4. What is God's best solution for self-pity?

5. Define any area of self-pity that you are habitually guilty of and ask God to forgive you and strengthen you in the future.

Notes

1. Marjorie Holmes, *To Help You Through the Hurting* (New York: Dobuleday, 1983).

2. *Julius Caesar,* Act iv, Scene III, lines 218-224.

8
Others Come in His Name

When I was a kid we waited everyday for old Sam to clomp past the field we played tag in. Sam, a hermit, lived back in the woods somewhere. There he sat, perched up on a rough slab of wood behind his only friend, a gray nag. Together they hauled a rotted wood cart full of junk from the town's dump. Rumor had it his wife had died giving birth to their first child, a stillborn son.

Now years later, Sam kept to himself. Not that anybody tried to get near. The stench from his tattered clothes held even the dogs back. But I remember how sad I felt for that old man when the kids threw rocks at his cart. Some hit his horse, and we'd hear squeals of laughter as she reared up as far as her stiff old bones enabled and bolted off to Sam's mumbled curses.

How I regret that I never stood up for Sam or stopped those rocks. But even in my grief for him, I let the chance go by to love him. Now Sam is gone, and so is love's ability to include one man. Now that I am a Christian, I have more to give those God sends across my path.

The secret is know God's love first. They say Mother Teresa closes her eyes and drinks in God's love even during interviews. No wonder she has so much to give. It must be heavenly love that put her arms around an old leper while she peeled his rags away from the sores. Reporters told us they had to leave the room for the stench, just like I left the scene when old Sam needed love.

But through Sam's life and Mother Teresa's devotion, I learned another small truth about love. It covers the differences, it comes from God's own heart, and it removes filthy rags. Only God's love will reach into another person deep enough to keep him. Only this love active in a person's life will woo the hurting ones back into the fold. And it alone will remove the filthy rags still hanging onto all our churches to release the treasures inside. When I give love to whoever crosses my path, others will stop and ask: "*Is it possible to be loved like that?*"

Some will be easy to love. But many, sent to us by God because they never knew love, are not.

Giving to others mysteriously helped me through rough waters in my own lonelier times. God promises that if we give to others, He will give to us (Luke 6:38).

I am not saying that when I feel lonely I should run out and give to make the feeling go away. It doesn't work that way. When you get home from "giving out," the feelings just come back.

But the habit of giving does bring joy to fight those lonely times when they sneak up. There is a difference! The first motive gives with the demand of immediate personal benefit. The latter patterns a habit of giving as taught in the Scripture and brings the promise of a greater reward that God has for the servant.

We all know what joy showered down when we helped somebody else. Our service turned the day into an adventure for everybody around. God mysteriously blossoms a person's own life when that person waters the seeds in many other gardens. But to love others means to serve them. Servants are hard to find today, but the call is still there.

These people are like the landing gear of good ideas already in flight. Persons who serve often have simple solutions for problems. They may not create the vision, but when they catch someone else's, it goes a step further to bring it to pass.

It took a creative mind to invent the first airplane. It took the dedicated service of Orville and Wilbur Wright for it to lift off the runway. In many attempts at Kitty Hawk, a vision was developed by two servants. Jesus gave us the example when He washed the disciples' feet.

Service may not always find a place in New York's Hall of Fame, but the rewards are real. Joy and fulfillment seem to follow the servant like a faithful puppy runs alongside his owner. Giving to others becomes an adventure in itself for the giver.

A servant acquires disciplines that others never see. Training is often tough at first. Sudden gusts of wind damaged the Wright brothers' gear and prevented flight for hundreds of trial runs. But on December 17, 1903, a 745-pound wheelless byplane nicknamed "The Flyer" climbed ten feet above the sand, carrying Orville into the 27-mile-per-hour wind toward success.

So where do you start? Mark Twain said: "Make it a point to do something every day that you don't want to do. This is the golden rule for acquiring the habit of doing your duty without pain." The Bible tells us that the servant who is faithful with little will be given much.

You may have to look hard to find examples today. It isn't popular to give without expecting any return, especially among the ones who already struggle with being single and with single parenting. But they are there. Just as 85 percent of the earth's greenery is found hidden under ocean waters, many true servants are not noticed at a glance.

A person who worries about "being used" will never know the servant's champion status. "He that is greatest among you shall be your servant," (Matt. 23:11, KJV).

But I am not a doormat! you may proclaim. Or you may think back to times when serving ultimately meant manipulation. That brings me to my next point.

Service is not servitude, which implies imposed work for a punishment or crime. But it gives for the sake of giving, wears a robe of cheer, and does not come with an open fist. It recognizes the higher and happier calling—servanthood—over being served.

As servants we reach up past the mundane act to the One we

serve: God. Not one of us would walk away from the kind of joy that adds strength to even a menial task and tackles challenges with greater success. Leo Tolstoy said:

> Joy can be real only if people look upon their life as a service, and have a definite object in life outside themselves and their personal happiness.

It won't be convenient to give out when you have so many needs yourself. Certainly the world doesn't teach us how. Some say that technology is to blame. Bank tellers, for example, are being replaced by computer tellers. All you have to do is drive up to the window and shove your plastic card into the machine, punch in a few numbers, and you've completed your banking. Helping others seems to be a thing of the past in some company training schools.

Service stations used to provide fuel, for instance, and maintenance for the car. Windshield cleaning and a few friendly facts of current events from the company's attendant were often thrown in. Often now service is reduced to a machine that tells you when you've pumped all you can afford and a computer to calculate payment for serving yourself. You may hear a muffled word of greeting under the plexiglass window that receives your cash, but usually you have to read lips to snap even that up before the next serve-yourself customer takes your place to pass his money through the slot.

Things used to be different. Feudal kings, for example, recognized the virtue of faithful service. They added the title "knight" to those who served faithfully in their kingdoms. In a public accolade, the king would touch his sword on the shoulder of a man, conferring knighthood on him in a special ceremony. Not only were a few men dubbed knights at court in connection with service but the servant everywhere took on a noble and timeless distinction in that role.

But how can a single person be a knight, you may ask? Shouldn't I wait until my own life is together before I try to help someone else? No, help others now, so together we can build God's kingdom on earth. He promises to be strong through our weakness. I quoted this promise to myself for the first five years I was alone until I began to believe it in my heart.

Everybody has a worthy cause to serve. There is always someone else who needs whatever a person has. And Scripture shows how to give it.

> And whoever wants to be first must be your slave—just as the Son of Man did not come to be served but to serve . . . (Matt. 20: 27).

How many of us ever consider a service left undone? Those little acts of kindness we omit, a tender word forgotten, an unmailed letter to a friend, a flower not picked, or a burden not lifted from a brother's shoulder may easily flee our minds. While one person claims, "I have enough trouble of my own," someone else carries heartache that awaits a brother's loving touch.

On the other hand, a simple kindness to some fellow struggler spreads wealth in much greater proportion than the energy spent in performing the service. And the author reaps fruit for his own life at the same time. While it is true, he may never pass that way again, he left it a better place for being there once.

A person's service will never be greater than the willingness to give without counting the cost. I know a widow who sold her house to pay the court costs for a teenage son who got tangled up with a biker's group and took part of their rap in a drug raid. When the case ended, that boy left the group and moved back home. Awed at such sacrificial, unconditional love the boy found a good job and vowed to pay every penny back. That was the end of his reckless involvements.

Service comes in different kinds of gift wrap, sizes, and shapes. I met a young woman who was on her own with three children the other day. She had lived with three different men with the same results: broken visions and crushed dreams. There was such an ache in my heart to carry her into the love of God that would last. But she was too suspicious of "false" promises for me to use words effectively.

I prayed silently, *Dear Lord, please direct me to Your path for this dear woman.* Then I remembered she said she had no family to support her and that she was moving in two weeks. So I told her I really wanted to help her in some way with the move.

"There was a problem with cleaning all the hardwood floors," my new friend shared. "I have to leave with the movers," she added.

That was it! "I'd love to wash and wax them," I told her. It wasn't that I like doing hardwood floors. But I did love hearing God's answer to my prayer and helping me to obey it.

His presence filled that empty apartment while Tanya and I scrubbed and polished. We prayed she would see Jesus through this unconditional help. Then I left a Bible on the counter when we left.

We were invited over to the new home for fellowship. I know God is going to use our small service as a bridge of love to pour in the gospel and make a way for His presence in this family. Already I have faith that the young mother's response to our help will be salvation.

Service often starts small, where ordinary people simply bloom where they are planted. In the small beginnings of a stucco-and-brick watch shop in Haarlem, Holland, Corrie Ten Boom, author of *The Hiding Place,* helped her father care for many adopted Ten Booms. They helped the Jews whenever they could, and Corrie held a club every afternoon from two to three o'clock for retarded adults others had no time for. These small everyday services prepared Corrie for years of suffering in German concentration camps later, where she became world famous for the hope and encouragement she brought to other war prisoners.

Until she died in 1983, this servant brought a message of hope to prisoners. She wrote best-selling books like *The Hiding Place, Tramp for the Lord,* and *Corrie Ten Boom's Prison Letters,* and she shared the faith that kept her going into her eighties.

Service wears its own price tag. Martin Luther King paid with his life. Bach gave his sight to leave some of the finest music ever written. And Gutenburg poured every penny he had into the printing press.

But whatever the cost, service becomes a priceless heirloom to its recipient while illuminating the servant, as "Invictus" proclaims:

> And everyday out of the dark night of suffering shine forth unconquerable souls. With lights so vivid they brighten the way for others.[1]

Bible Study Suggestions

Thessalonians 1:2-10; Luke 21:4; Acts 4:36-37

Practical Applications

1. How can a single person help others? (1 Thess. 1:2-10).
2. How could one poor widow help others? (Luke 21:4).
3. How did Joseph help the apostles? (Acts 4:36-37).
4. Who do you know that needs your help?
5. What little or much could you offer to them that God could multiply?

Notes

1. Holmes, *To Help You*

9

One Key for Happiness

Helen Keller once said that life is either a daring adventure, or it is nothing. But how often do you look for the challenge that hides behind every ordinary day's routines.

Friends can be a great blessing. Those few people who will leave footprints on our hearts often help prevent the doldrums. But some people drop friendships when a problem arises rather than try to mend the shattering bonds. Remember, you have to dare to take the risk of loving again. Do you have the faith to believe there are still people who want to love you? If so, you'll find a gold mine of others looking, too.

Charlie Brown might have had the single parent in mind when he said: "I need all the friends I can get." But Mark Twain caught the heart of friendship in *The Adventures of Tom Sawyer*. Tom was having a bad day. He felt rather lonely and rejected until he ran into Joe Harper, who had bigger problems. Joe's crisis was that he had been whipped in error. His mother had accused him of drinking cream he knew nothing about. The problem became the very thing that brought two friends together in empathy.

> Just at this point he met his soul's sworn comrade, Joe Harper—hard-eyed, and with evidently a great and dismal purpose in his heart. Plainly here were "two souls with but a single thought."
> . . .
> As the two boys walked sorrowing along, they made a new com-

pact to stand by each other and be brothers and never separate till death relieved them of their troubles. Then they began to lay their plans.

You may shout back, "Love may be good to you, Ellen, but not one person loves me." Or maybe a counterfeit love used you, then left you bleeding, ripped apart, and broken. Tragic stories seep out of even Christian circles. No matter where it lurks, selfish love manipulates, exploits, robs, and then deserts its victim.

Have you been disillusioned by love only given to get something in return? Maybe love was withheld as a cruel form of punishment when you didn't obey. Remember, God loves you with no conditions. You are never turned away by His love. You'll never meet rejection. Not that pain, disappointments, and tragedies won't strike. But watch what recognition of God's love does in the midst of difficulties.

So take the risk. Love God: let Him love you, and you'll soon find yourself loving others vulnerably again.

Friendship was a "sheltering tree" to Samuel Coleridge. A person willing to hang in through the storms will get to know the kind of relationships Alice met when she pursued the white rabbit down the rabbit hole. We will meet kings and queens, duchesses and March hares, if we cross the walls of trials and nurture friendships.

Maintaining good relationships, however, requires ongoing effort. I found there were areas where I was too sensitive and got hurt too easily. Learning to accept the fact that I was wrong helped me over many hurdles.

Another problem I took to single parenthood was the habit of blaming others for my unhappiness. It took a few years before I saw that only I am responsible for my happiness and God will never withhold joy from me when I need it. So with that I had to learn to shrug off hurts quickly and go back to the Lord for joy to walk on.

I learned that by applying a few basic principles, I found more happiness in relationships:

1. *Get to know your Friend and let Him know you* (John 15:15).

An acclaimed actress refused or could not open her heart to others. She lived and died alone. Having locked out her friends, she prevented entrance to the ones who would have comforted her. It was said of her that she found it difficult to talk about herself. At some times, it was painful. In many instances, she was too ashamed. At other times, she tried to maintain a mystery about herself, a reserve, a defense, so that people would not find out her vulnerable qualities and, with this knowledge, hurt her.

A lasting friendship cannot build on closed hearts. There must be clear, direct, honest communication between friends. Yes, we must make ourselves vulnerable and then work through the hurts that come. That is all part of the chord that binds strong union.

2. *Love unconditionally* (Prov. 17:17).

Let your friend know you care about her regardless of what she does. Affirm her often and tell her that she is important to you just as she is.

This is especially important between a parent and teenager. Studies have shown that where there is unconditional love and much affirmation, the friendships formed are deep and lasting. Take advantage of important moments like her return home after a weekend away to assure her. You might say, "I sure am glad to see you. Things just weren't the same when you were gone." There was no particular good thing that brought your love, just the return home!

3. *Support and encourage* (Eccl. 4:9-10; Job 2:11-13).

This may involve being there or just listening. Or it could call you to weep with your friend. Any touch, even an arm around the shoulders often shouts louder than words.

There are too many who go around correcting people for every tiny slip. Did you ever need a word of encouragement and end up getting corrected? When your friend is down tell him he's going to come through. Whenever a chance pops up, bless him.

4. *Be sensitive* (Prov. 26:18-19).

Only use caring words with your friend. Familiarity will breed contempt if your conversations break down to insults or careless nit-picking. Look beyond what is going on and ask the Holy Spirit to show you where your friend might need a sensitive ear. Then try to hear where he is coming from, not where you think he is.

Evelyn Christenson, in her book *Lord, Change Me!,* told of a critical discovery she made for all her interpersonal relationships. Her revelation is summed up in this powerful prayer for sensitivity to those closest to her:

> Lord, change me—don't change my husband, don't change my children, don't change my pastor, change me!

This attitude will revolutionize a friendship!

5. *Be loyal* (Prov. 16:28; 17:9).

Stand by your friend in every situation and take up his case before any accusers. This does not mean that you jeopardize your integrity for a friend or go against God's principles. Thomas à Becket defied his closest friend King Henry II over a matter of conscience. The King, once Becket's loyal supporter, decided to establish the throne's unchallenged supremacy over the church. The Archbishop of Canterbury's courage and conviction for "the liberty of God's church" broke their friendship and cost his own life.

The chief cupbearer was not loyal to Joseph when he forgot him. Delilah was not loyal to Samson but betrayed him. When you make a promise, however small, to a friend, keep that word at any cost. That is loyalty. If you forget and the friend reminds you, then you have a choice. But if you humble yourself and make good on that word, a sovereign strength and joy is poured into the friendship. Both will feel Christ's touch. That is sincerity and love in action.

6. *Tell the truth, even when it might hurt* (Prov. 27:6).

It will be easier to say, "You did a great job," when your friend asks you how his terrible speech was. But this is no help. Yet, neither would, "It was the most boring thing I've ever heard." Why not make a time and have him over. Sit down to go over it step by step. Be sure to list a number of positives before the negatives. You can always find something to praise, even if it was the shoes he wore. The truth you bring in love will become his stepping-stone to growing in whatever area you share.

7. *Be available to help* (Prov. 27:9).

Psychiatrists tell us there are many people who go to great lengths just to be heard and understood. But there is also a place, after hearing, to offer a word of wise counsel. If you have heard and understood, your words can bring freedom and joy to your friend.

Then, there is one thing left to be done. Seal his words with strict confidence! Such vulnerable encounters will not easily stand any gossip.

8. *Humble yourself in every clash* (Prov. 27:17; Phil. 2:1-11).

I recently saw a friendship break up because one very mature Christian would not humble herself and ask forgiveness. The younger Christian apologized many times but that was not enough glue for the relationship. The older Christian quietly took the position that she had done everything to show love and the other one just didn't know how to receive it. The relationship has had a breach since that day and has never been completely restored. As long as the older Christian denies her own sin, there is no hope for that friendship to grow any further.

We need to be quick to humble ourselves and take every word a friend brings to us seriously. If he says I hurt him, I hurt him. The Lord wants me to humble myself and ask his forgiveness. A relationship that goes past this hurdle will be a vulnerable and distinct one. It will reach mountaintops that the quitters will never see. You might even be right. It doesn't matter. Humble yourself, ask forgiveness, and watch what God will do with that friendship!

9. *Don't swallow hurts* (1 Cor. 13).

We are not to take personal injury out of anything that comes against us. If a friend rejects you, let God turn it around. It can become an ingredient for love. Let it send you running into the arms of Christ until He gives you the grace to go to your friend in love. Or you may have enough grace to let it drop and go on.

10. *Lay down your life* (John 15:13).

Only those willing to work at it can maintain their friendships. Are you willing to give your own life for the ones you love? The first step, Paul referred to in 1 Corinthians 10:24: "Let no man seek his own, but every man another's wealth" (KJV).

In the obituary Martin Luther King wrote for himself, he summed up the attitude a real friend has toward others:

Tell them I tried to feed the hungry,
Tell them I tried to clothe the naked,
Tell them I tried to help somebody.

Are you are in the middle of a shattering friendship? Take heart! It may take two to destroy the bond between friends, but one can reconnect that relationship with a much stronger cord. Begin today to bless your friend, and watch the joy pour in as strength.

Bible Study Suggestions

Luke 10:38-42; John 11:1-46; Matthew 27:55-61; 28:1-8; Luke 20:11-18; Job 2:11-13

Practical Applications

1. Who were some of Jesus' best friends?

Answers: Luke 10:38-42; John 11:1-46; Matthew 27:55-61; 28:1-8; Luke 20:11-18

2. Describe Job's three friends.

Answer: Job 2:11-13.

3. Name the person who has helped you most in life. What were his or her main qualities?

4. Ask the Lord to point out who you are to get involved with and make it a family affair to love them as Christ loved. Discuss the progress at family devotions.

10
The Christian Community Needs You

When I first met Brenda in May 1980, she sat in a tilted-back wheelchair, as her head rested in a metal brace. Two friends carried her up the stairs to our home fellowship from a rented van.

Brenda's battle with a dystonic neurological disorder had little to do with the deep friendship that grew between us. But I do know that as she trusted God through surgery after surgery, I saw the living faith of Christ in my friend. Brenda became my best example of what it meant to give.

Her disease progressed until intense muscle spasms dislocated her hips. The spasms attacked her throat until she could barely swallow. But Brenda always had a few words to encourage me whenever I dropped by the hospital. The time came when she had to sign papers to allow her spine to be severed to prevent the spasms. Shortly after that operation which paralyzed Brenda from the waist down, she told me, "I pray daily that my life will be an instrument used to bring others closer to Christ." And it does. Brenda gave me something no other person could: She showed me faith in action. And I will never lose that gift.

Recently, at age twenty-seven, she said, "Although my life has not been easy, I have many things to enjoy and experience. With my illness I do not know what tomorrow holds. But then, who does? I only want to know that when today is gone, I can honestly say that I have lived up to my full potential.

My gift to Brenda is far too small. But this treasure in one earthen vessel, my friend, brought a priceless gift to me as she showed God's faithfulness. Just by the way she laughed at little things and glossed over the negatives, I saw Christ. And Brenda listened with an active mind. She really cared how my week had gone. Because Brenda knew God's love, she gave it out as naturally as some people shake hands. While her gifts are unique, Brenda has developed them through faithful use.

But what could I give, you might say? Or worse, you may compare your small gift to the "higher" talents in your church.

When the 700th unsuccessful attempt to develop the incandescent light threw Thomas Edison's assistants into despair, he said, "Don't call it a mistake; call it an education. Now we know 700 things not to do."

We all make mistakes, plenty of them. Not one of us is immune. But why not let the wipeouts become part of your next attempt to give?

A sixteen-year study of 350,000 people found four out of five have jobs that don't match their abilities. It suggests the tests we use do not adequately predict what gifts a person has. But with God's help a person can discover and confirm these gifts. They are often not the abilities we take credit for. But these capacities God places in each of us offers us the choice to give back to God and to help build in His kingdom.

Too many make the grave mistake to bury what God gave them.

> Find out what God would have you do
> And do that little well
> For what is great and what is small
> The Lord alone can tell
>
> —Author Unknown

Not that you'll meet fast success every time. Abraham Lincoln met a business failure in 1833. He suffered a nervous breakdown in 1836. Then in 1848 Lincoln lost renomination to Congress. In

1854 he missed nomination for US president and lost the Senate race again in 1858.

But when Lincoln became president in 1860, he led the country with unusual courage and compassion. The fact that Lincoln failed often taught him the most important lessons he could have as leader of a country.

Somebody out there needs your gift, whatever state it's in. So dare to risk failure. Dare to be vulnerable or even to fail somebody you love. The joy of spreading God's gifts for others to enjoy will make up for the disappointments.

While it's never fun to be let down by Christians, these are the ones God chooses to visit us through over and over. When I am let down, I have learned to say, "Father, You let that happen. I'll trust You in it until I can understand why."

Job was let down on every front, and then came the last straw. Job's own wife told him to just curse God for it and take the consequences. But like Job we need to say, "Shall we accept good from God and not trouble?"

The key is forgive, forgive, and forgive.

Forgive the friend who cuts you off because she's afraid you'll steal her husband. Forgive the husband who pats you on the back and tells you how suffering is good for you in the long run. One woman told me, "We'd invite you for Christmas dinner, but you might as well face your situation now." Forgive, forgive, and forgive. Then love again quickly.

Sometimes the ones you were sure would stand beside you turn away. Friends you opened up to most vulnerably may drop you in your loneliest times. But you will find your deepest and most intimate friends there in the body of Christ. And just when you think you're most alone, one will pop up and ask you over.

Never with any other group did Tanya and I find such friendship, love, and understanding as we find in the body of Christ. While God could move on any heart to come alongside, He seems to prefer Christians to be His ambassadors most of the time.

Just like good families support and care about each one, so the body of Christ must carry the Father's love one to another. We tend to think of giving extravagant things that few ever attain. Why not start with a little gift of loving somebody just because they need you. You won't go far before you'll spot just the one who needs your love. But notice how that gift you give becomes the very instrument that roots you into a fellowship.

It took me years to see this principle. Perhaps that is because it's not the kind of thing you see overnight. You have to commit yourself to His family in order to really be a part of it. And give. Don't expect others to give all the time. Give back, especially to those who are lonely or hurting. You'll find love comes back in the most surprising ways.

One thing I missed most was the regularity of family life. Then my dearest friend asked me over on a regular basis, and I looked forward all week to that event.

Then I found, you have to be willing to hang in even when it hurts. You have to stay and let God work tough situations out. This was hard for me! My background was logical thinking and debate. So when I ran into obstacles, I threw my skills into gear and came up with "fair" conclusions. When they didn't work, I went into a tailspin and withdrew.

But God was relentless in being "fair" according to my rules. I lost some powerful games before I saw a glimpse of His higher principles. For awhile I felt like I was running through a mine field without the map while God was shaping my attitude. Every time a bomb went off under my feet, it hurt.

Then one day I realized that God was preparing me for bigger faith. Through some broken promises and shattered dreams He was lifting my eyes up to see the One who would never leave me or turn His back on me. When I saw this, I found it easier to forgive myself for letting others down and to forgive others when they failed me. God uses each thing that happens in the Christian community to stretch us and mold us. There was a time when I became bitter and held grudges. Now I find it easier to tell God how I feel and quickly forgive the person. For me this was a slow process, and still I fail at times. But He remains a patient Teacher! Remember, forgiveness means we love again as if it never happened. If you won't, you have not forgiven. That was a bitter lesson for me. As long as it hurt, I had to keep forgiving. Then one day, the hurt disappeared, and I hugged that woman again.

And His blessings far outweigh His discipline. Just as with any good parent, love motivates both.

Christian communities, either church or school, often fill in the gaps that a single-parent home makes for your child. When families get together or kids go fishing with Dad, your child gets invited. There is cooperation between parents for having the kids over and driving them places.

Then when Tanya was at camp or away, I found that our Christian community became a haven for a lonely evening or a chat. Just as in a family you are free to drop by, God makes that provision for His children.

Others call me when they need time, and I find that He makes it possible for me to reach out to help others the way I've been helped so often.

A dear friend who helped me through the roughest time gave me just the right book to read when I hit bottom. For special occasions he'd send a thought God laid on his heart, and it spoke right into mine. One such plaque still hangs near my desk, "Be strong and of good courage . . . for it is the Lord your God who goes with you; he will not fail you or forsake you" (Deut. 31:6, RSV).

This friend always said it like it was. Anybody can compliment you, say something to tickle your ears. But a very rare friend cares enough to say, "You've let self-pity in. Get back on track!" Only a few will understand where you are and offer a hand when you're down. But learn to hold on to God as your best Friend, and He'll walk you through when others let go.

I know I'll fail people, and I know I will get let down by others.

One friend said to me, "Ellen, you were not very compassionate with me until you went through the same pain." This was quite a shock because I felt I had really loved that person. But I see now that I could not understand rejection until I was deeply rejected. I could not understand loneliness until I was left alone in pain. How could I enter into my friend's deep water while mine was so shallow and protected.

Those are the times when we learn an important principle in the Christian life: *you will never know you can hold onto God alone until there is nothing left to hold onto but God alone.*

This thought prevents a person from bitterness in the face of discouragement, and it helps promote love and trust without an unhealthy dependence on others. I give because God gave to me, and I look to Him only for my supply to keep on giving. Not that mutual giving won't happen in groups. But unreasonable expectations break even the strongest relationships and put others in bondage. Better to expect little and give much. Then, when a little surprise comes your way, you'll be delighted. And the Lord will see to it that surprises come.

Remember you are special, and there are no others just like you. C. S. Lewis said, "There are no ordinary people. You have never talked to a mere mortal." It's true. You can give to a group things no other person can. Believe it or not, your appearance, voice, intelligence, habits, and personal tastes all make you one of a kind. Nobody else can make your fingerprint. God designed gifts for you to share with others that will bring excitement and joy into your life in the giving. But nobody will force them from you. It's your choice: to hide and lose your gifts or to spread and develop them.

Bible Study Suggestions

2 Timothy 4:9-21; 1 Corinthians 13; Romans 12:6

Practical Applications

1. Describe Paul's good friends: (2 Tim. 4:9-18).

2. Discuss the attitudes we should have in relationships: (1 Cor. 13).

3. What difficulties do you have in a present relationship with which you have struggled?

4. Apply 1 Corinthians 13 to the difficult relationship to check your own attitudes. Can you see any that you could change? Be specific. (Ask the Lord's guidance.)

5. Many people make the grave mistake of burying their gifts, so others never see them. What things do you do well? What do you best? See Romans 12:6.

11
Safe in God's Arms

Whenever we jump into our Father's arms, He catches us and holds us up. But sometimes we are like the timid child, afraid to jump from the side of the pool into a father's waiting arms.

A person's reluctance at first may be justified. Somebody who was painfully disappointed as a child by a derelict human father often shies away from trust.

After a church picnic a few days ago, we all trooped over to see six newborn chicks. After one peek, a few of the kids scurried to the top of a nine-foot hayloft. One boy yelled, "Let's jump!" and then it was, "Hey, Dad, can you catch us?"

Excited shrieks followed three-year-old Peter who, like his namesake the apostle Peter, lept without thinking twice into his father's arms. The way Peter hurled his little body up into the air for the flight and giggled, you knew he was sure of a secure landing.

But then came Darren. When everybody cheered him on, he stepped boldly to the edge, poised to dive. Then, after second thoughts, Darren moved back. A parent finally lifted him under the arms, past the bails, so Darren dropped laughing into his father's hands. Joey, a suntanned four-year-old, was next. He cried when the boys coaxed him to the edge. And three-year-old Josh sat well back so he could take in the whole ceremony. Josh's expression told us he had no intention of even coming near the edge.

What a picture of our reactions! Sometimes we step up and almost jump into His arms when we need His security. At other times we cry and run away from our Father's love. But when we hurl ourselves into the air, knowing He will never step aside but can be trusted to catch us, God is free to teach us more about trust. Each time a person lands safely with Him, that person is reassured of those everlasting arms underneath. Just like Peter, who had jumped so many times and learned more about the faithful care of his father, we learn to depend on His being there.

Whose arms do you run into when things get you down? When you are afraid? There is a place of comfort for each lonely one of us where we find rest and strength.

Perhaps Job was looking into the future, anticipating a bumper sticker like: "Have You Hugged Your Child Today?" when he said: "I have heard many things like these; miserable comforters are you all!" (Job 16:2).

You may have a family's arms of acceptance, or a partner sent by God to love and shelter you. Or you may be alone without any outside support. Whatever your state, married or single, you are welcome in God's love.

If that seems impossible, let me share a prayer that may help you.

> Lord, I believe
> In the sun, even when
>   it is behind the clouds;
> In the seed, even when
>   it lies unsprouted under the ground;
> In faith, even when I have been betrayed;
> In love, even when I have been rejected;
> In hope, even when I have been hurt;
> In God, even when
>   You do not answer my prayers.
> Amen.
>
> —Author Unknown

Each person has the choice. Do I choose my Father's arms or

do I choose to journey alone, as a nomad under the scorching heat and waiting vultures of the desert. There was a time when I chose the latter. My only hope was that God might send a partner one day to rescue me out of my loneliness. I did not accept God's deep intimate friendship.

Then one night as I was praying after a particularly taxing session of counseling a broken marriage, God sent His intimate presence to me in a most remarkable way. I was struck with the sense of His holiness, like I have never been before. Immediately, I saw that I would never have the ability to be holy like He was. But I could enter into that holiness, just like I could enter into His presence. Waves of comfort passed over me that night for fifteen minutes, and I knew that God was showering His love out on this tired single parent. (It has often happened that when I was busy giving out to another, God came to help me, as in this case). The revelation that stayed was His invitation to come to Him at any-time and to expect His love and comfort.

So why don't we go to Him more?

One of the reasons we don't always run into God's arms is that we have created in our minds a picture of a harsh and distant God who does not care about us intimately. A person will not run to a taskmaster. Can you imagine wanting a cruel stranger's arms around you? You'd rather be alone. So until I grew to know who God really was, I did not really welcome His friendship. But once I saw the real God of His Word, how I loved to be with Him. You will, too. You'll tell Him your deepest needs, and you'll run to Him faster when loneliness strikes.

Perhaps that is why the devil wants us to see the unfair God He described to Eve in the garden. That way he can keep us from going to our Father when we need Him most.

When Picasso said that every act of creation is first of all an act of destruction, he saw the need to tear down old thinking patterns and make room for the new. The Bible tells us that if you try to pour new wine into old skins, the skins will burst. You need new wineskins, Jesus reminded the disciples.

While it helps to have memories from a dad who held you and cared, it isn't necessary. God will both love and comfort you!

How Can I Run into God's Arms?

1. See God as He really is.

For some of us, our traditions dictated a cold God who punished quickly and did not love much. But God is not like that. Isaiah gave an accurate picture of who God is when he said:

> He tends his flock like a shepherd:
> > He gathers his lambs in his arms
> and carries them close to his heart;
> > he gently leads those that have
> > young (40:11).

The best a cold, distant image of God can bring is a congregation of Pharisees who criticize others out of the coldness of their own hearts. They neither have a personal relationship with God, nor do they submit to Him for their daily living. They put on church like a garment, then leave it at the door with the benediction. Jesus called them a "brood of vipers" and hypocrites who resembled "whitewashed tombs" (Matt. 23:27-33).

2. Be ready to repent and change.

God cannot separate Himself from His holiness. He will ask us to change in any sinful areas of our lives whenever we spend time with Him. But He will always bless us when we obey.

When we are caught up in relationship with a living God, we are free to love others without judging them. We draw our love from the One who never changes in His perfect love for us, and we give out of that love. So even forgiveness comes easier when we understand our position in God.

A person in right relationship to God wants to please Him. I have seen depression beaten when a person decides to follow God rather than giving in to feelings. Even when disappointment or rejection comes, there is a safe place inside the everlasting arms of the Savior.

Only there are tears wiped away, forgiveness found, and hearts restored. There we get our guidance as well as the strength to carry on in tough places.

I planned to take a sabbatical after twenty years of teaching high school with no break, and I had a modest nest egg in the small house I owned. My prayers assured me that God was calling me to write, so I took the quantum leap—only to watch the market drop and my reserve wash away. Here I stood with no job, no money, and a house sold with $300 owing the bank. Fear and depression fought for a place in my heart, and at times they found comfortable lodging there.

But the Lord began to teach me how to hide in Him. I was always concerned that our friends would have to take on the burdens of our financial lack. So the Lord comforted me by encouraging me in prayer to come to Him alone for every need and spend time in prayer rather than telling people. "If George Mueller could believe in You alone to provide housing for thousands of orphaned children, I can look to You for one," I prayed.

By consciously remaining in His arms through the hurdles, I escaped pity parties and gripe groups. It was a lesson to me in the joys found in His presence. That Christmas I could only give my teenage daughter a pair of barrettes. But we had a wonderful time together. In our little He became so much more! Then just after Christmas, a small check for an article I wrote for a local paper came unexpectedly. We jumped on a ferry, bought a hot dog each, and went to see a Walt Disney special in a neighboring city. He provided for even an extra Christmas treat in His time. By now I was becoming much more accustomed to waiting in His arms for my supply. And a few times He's sent a dear friend to me just at that lowest point. When you look to God, He'll send His own best friends your way. One friend in particular often carried God's own love to us in every practical way.

Battles are often won by God when we step off the field and rest in Him. That's why God instructed Jehoshaphat (2 Chron. 20) to stand still, rest, and see His deliverance take place. In our sense of "fair" deals, we often come out swinging. But God isn't "fair" by our standards. It wasn't fair that Joseph went to jail at his employer's whim. But it was the place where God trained him for a great ministry. Joseph could have never withstood all the rejection and then blame from a seducing woman unless he knew how to run to God and hide in Him.

Recently, I was speaking at a singles retreat. Many young people there admitted to throwing their lives into neutral in order to find a mate. What a waste of years! God holds out His arms to His children to bring them close and bless them, and they run in the opposite direction looking for a mate before He sends one. It broke God's heart when the Israelites would not look to Him but insisted on a human king to rule over them. So it must be with singles who refuse His love.

Sadder yet, God gave Israel their king. And if we beg He'll give a mate before the best time. But we may be sacrificing more than we know. We may lose the most valuable time we'll ever have to be held lovingly in the arms of the One who loves perfectly. A person may be looking and running while God longs for one who will wait and receive His love first.

A person who learns to accept all the rich comfort of God in tranquil times, in the silence of His presence will carry this strength to all life's trials. Too many problems found me spiritually impoverished before I learned this.

God did not club me when I neglected my morning meditation, but I ran into trouble every time. Like the night I stayed up to finish reading a George MacDonald novel. There was barely time to get Tanya off to school the next morning. My car ran out of gas on the way, and the telephone made demands for most of the afternoon.

It was late that night before I admitted to God where the real problem lay.

I took my Bible off to the little park by our house and poured out my wounded heart to God. He was so gentle and good in His words to me that day. He says in 2 Peter 3 that we are to do our best to be in peace when trouble strikes.

Paul speaks of the "God of all comfort" (2 Cor. 1:3, KJV). He comforts each one in all our afflictions to make us capable of comforting other people when they need it. So we let God love us and then pass it on.

Did you ever think of the strong movement of love generated by the Trinity? The bond between the Father, Son, and Holy Spirit is love! This love is ours when we come to God. He loves you as much as He loves Jesus, His own Son.

A man will run from a woman who goes after him with the idea of "catching" him. Too many lose what could have been a rich friendship because they want a mate.

Why not cling to God instead. Then trust Him to bring that relationship. Not that I'm suggesting you stay home and stagnate. Just the opposite. A person who trusts God is free to walk into any circle. He or she mixes with all kinds: men and women. And that person is more likely to have those encounters with the opposite sex that every single person needs.

I once dated a man who constantly talked about his need to have a family again. Just like men who run from pushy women, I ran from him in fear. A good friendship got lost because this man would not run to God for his security. And I knew I could not provide what he wanted. So I stepped back before he got hurt.

Perhaps God reserves one section of our hearts for His friendship alone. When the bottom falls out of a friendship, you always know whose arms provide unconditional love and security.

My experience taught me that even when all else fails, I remains safe in my Father's arms. How often I've thanked Him for that privilege.

Bible Study Suggestions

Psalm 91; 2 Corinthians 1:3-4; 1 Thessalonians 4:18

Practical Applications

1. How can we comfort one another? See 1 Thessalonians 4:18 and 1 Corinthians 1:4.

2. Memorize Psalm 91:

He who dwells in the shelter of the Most High will rest in the
   shadow of the Almighty.
I will say of the Lord, "He is my refuge and my fortress,
   my God, in whom I trust."

Surely he will save you from the fowler's snare and from the deadly
   pestilence.
He will cover you with his feathers,
   and under his wings you will find refuge;
   his faithfulness will be your shield and rampart.
   You will not fear the terror of night
   nor the arrow that flies by day,
   nor the pestilence that stalks in the darkness,
   nor the plague that destroys at midday.
A thousand may fall at your side,
   ten thousand at your right hand,
   but it will not come near you.
   You will only observe with your eyes
   and see the punishment of the wicked.

If you make the Most High your dwelling—
   even the Lord, who is my refuge—
   then no harm will befall you,
   no disaster will come near your tent.
   For he will command his angels concerning you
   to guard you in all your ways;
   they will lift you up in their hands,
   so that you will not strike your foot against a stone.
   You will tread upon the lion and the cobra;
   you will trample the great lion and the serpent.

"Because he loves me," says the Lord, "I will rescue him;
    I will protect him, for he acknowledges my name.
    He will call upon me, and I will answer him;
    I will be with him in trouble,
    I will deliver him and honor him.
    With long life will I satisfy him
    and show him my salvation."

12
Kids Can Make It Work

If you have children, you can involve your kids in the adventure of walking alone with God. They, too, learn to trust in God for everything they need. But if you exclude them in your faith walk, you will rob them of a close relationship with their Father. After all, He is head of their lives too.

I know a Christian couple who entertained believers in their home for months at a time. They got to know people from all over the world and still visit some of the missionaries they took in. But their five children were not involved, except to lose their beds every time a family came. Even though all the children walk with God today, one married girl told me, "I will never have people stay in my home for more than a few days. I resented all the Christian families my parents took in when I was little." How sad. Now her boys will never benefit from the fellowship of God's family on an intimate level in the home.

Another family decided that their children should never give up their beds for guests. So they always put children first and let them know that nobody else would ever occupy that place. Their house guests could stay for short periods, but the kids always knew and openly admitted to their friends: *We will always be first.*

I was giving a seminar on *agape love,* and a woman in her nineties wheeled her chair up to the front afterward to tell me her story. Her parents simply loved people. That included their children. But the children were in on every family offering. She told me how their parents slept on the floor more than once, so a tired missionary couple could have a retreat. And the children gave up their things and even their rooms. Then they'd gather around after the company left and pray that God would bless their little gifts of love to that person. Although they had very little themselves, she said, "I'll never forget how I learned to give sacrificially from watching my godly parents."

"When I was a little girl on the farm in Saskatchewan during the depression," she said, "I had very old shoes. Then one day my parents bought me a pair of shiny, brown leather shoes. They were my pride and joy," she told me. "But one day a little girl came to our house with dirty shabby clothes and no shoes. My mother told me to give the girl my new shoes, and I did. They fit her perfectly."

Then she told me how she put the ends of the rolled oats box in her old shoes to cover up the holes. But she learned from her mother about the adventure of giving the best away.

My question is this: "What if God says to put a poor family first one day and let your own family wait?" If God is really first, that is enough. He will show the rest. And He'll never ask you to leave your family unloved while you love somebody else. But I have seen families never really get past their own very intimately. What a pity.

Did you ever watch the face of an elderly person when you took a minute to stop and talk? Or notice the expression on a casual friend's face when you reserve time for him or her? Why not involve the mentally or physically handicapped, who often get left out?

Remember, *when you put others first, God seems to shine His face on you in a special way.* So everybody involved gets loved!

When Tanya and I teamed up to put others first, we watched a few big miracles happen. I've always had a problem with the teaching: "Put God first, then your partner, then your kids, then your job, and then the church." Let's face it. After all the "your's," how much room is left? We are self-centered by nature, and our times encourage self-seeking.

Now when I teach on this subject, I tell parents: put your children before yourself! Then put others first together with your children. That seems to work for us, and I see it in the Scriptures. In effect I had been putting myself first, then my children came before everybody else. That order invites selfishness and greed. Not only that, how could Tanya ever learn to love with this poor example. So I prayed, "Lord, You are first. Please help me now to put myself after Tanya." And He did work a miracle.

My tendency was to concentrate on my future, my problems, and all the hurdles a single parent runs every day. Tanya was only one spoke in my wheel of confusion. That's before I rearranged my priorities one Easter Sunday.

An extraordinary event where one rather ordinary man put himself last showed me a new dimension of God's love. The whole church stood silent and awed at one man's attempt to put others first. That scene changed my priority list, and I scratched out Ellen and rewrote: "Tanya." It happened on Easter Sunday when I needed help. Being all Tanya had for family was too much responsibility. Big holidays smacked of families, and I dreaded them. So I walked into church with a heavy heart.

The little church's aisles swelled with the Easter gathering until there were no more pews to squeeze into. Both the organ and the piano harmonized "He is risen" a few extra times while the deacons lined the last chairs from the church hall along the back of the sanctuary. A few more latecomers shuffled down the side aisles and leaned against the wall.

Then I noticed Andy. His smile beamed with a sense of Easter joy until he saw his spot in the back row was filled. Nobody in the congregation ever sat there because it was common knowledge: Andy would arrive from the mentally handicaped home late and sit in the back row.

Confusion masked Andy's face now as the congregation stood

to open the service, and he had no place to sit. With the simplicity with which Andy did everything, he made his way up the center aisle to a large clearing just below the platform. There the ministers and choir members stood poised to open the service. Andy lowered his huge body to the floor at the first amen, crossing his legs Indian style.

In the pause that seated the congregation, another man, a deacon in the church for many years, left his place in the pew and started slowly up the center aisle toward Andy. It took Marvin a long time to reach the front. Perhaps it was out of respect for this eighty-year-old servant, much loved by all of us, or maybe it was sheer curiosity that brought that hushed silence over the whole church. Even the minister gripped the sides of the podium and watched.

Slowly Marvin shifted his lean frame onto the cane and lowered his aged body to the floor beside Andy.

With tears in his eyes, the minister closed the Bible over his sermon notes.

"Our sermon has just been preached," he said. "The Lord would speak one further word to the rest of us: 'Whatever you did for the humblest of my brothers you did for me' " (Matt. 25:40, Phillips).

Yet too often, I didn't recognize Christ in my own daughter. By putting her last, I lost every opportunity to rebuild our home.

Jesus washed His disciples' feet to show us the leader's service to weaker ones. By doing this He built an intimate relationship with His friends. Whenever we wash our childrens' feet, we strengthen the bonds between weak and strong. Another thing I noticed is that we can tackle anything when others count more.

When I put Tanya first, I found there were many things she could do for the family. Each person has a gift. No matter how small, it will fill a need when it is used. Tanya often came in bubbling when I took on too many pressures. After four or five of her corny jokes, we often found a lighter atmosphere in the kitchen while dinner cooked. Instead of complaining about my pressures, I listened to her humor. We both won!

Put your children before yourself, and you'll find you respect them like you would a person of highest rank. Think of the child as Christ in disguise, and you will not talk down to him or condescend. Nor will you allow behaviour that will destroy Christ's life within him.

Ask questions about your child's interests, for instance. I asked Tanya to show me what she worked on in art classes. And I talked about her friends. As I hit topics she enjoyed, I opened the door for her to share intimately. Then I listened actively to every response. What a difference from a few months earlier where she found few gaps in my schedule to make any mark. You'll be amazed at some very highly sensitive and developed skills your child has. Then ask to see her project or to hear more about her interest. Look around for a chance to visit an art gallery together, or help with a social project. But get involved. This was the basis of better communication for Tanya and me.

Give unconditionally without expecting any return, and you'll be surprised how love comes back. Samuel Coleridge said that friendship is a sheltering tree. It can also be a citadel of refuge in a family.

Gradually, I replaced my anxieties for Tanya's welfare with regular prayer. Even though we were together, quite often I put her high on my prayer list.

Almost every day I prayed: "Dear Lord, please put Your arms safely around Tanya. Then do whatever You want with her." This prayer brought faith to my thoughts about Tanya. I gained trust in the Lord to take good care of her.

On other occasions I had no idea how to pray. "You know the beginning from the end, Lord," I often said. "Please help me to pray the right prayers for Tanya." The Bible assures us the Holy Spirit will guide us in our prayers, and I took this promise at face value when I came up short.

Ask God to show you how your child thinks, feels, and responds.

Listen to any hint showing past events that need healing. Then pray for these areas specifically.

Continually lead your children toward Jesus. Don't encourage too much leaning, or you will have very dependent children who will either follow you instead of Christ or leave you worn out. It can be very dangerous to play God in anybody's life, especially your children's lives.

It takes time and effort to teach a child how to have a daily devotional life of prayer and Bible study. But this will pay back a hundredfold in dividends. One of the greatest joys of my life came when Tanya set her alarm an hour early morning after morning to make time for the Lord before her day got going. Give plenty of room for failure. After all, you make big mistakes. And God will often use a person's weakness to show His strength.

Not that you renege from your part. Some children find the Bible hard to read at first, for instance. You may want to get your children an easier version, one that has a few illustrations. Then work through the routine with them for a week or so until they understand. Some families stay at the dinner table, read a passage, and then discuss.

Tanya and I talk about the Lord often in an average day, although she has her own devotions. Even after that, ask the children often how it is going and encourage a discussion on some of their Bible study topics. Pray with them over areas of concern or failure. And never allow a personal time with the Lord to replace your family devotional periods.

When I encouraged Tanya to fellowship with other girls her age, I found she grew and stretched. Having a friend over was something we had to plan in advance. My hectic schedule could not stand the strain of too many sudden surprises. But Tanya understood this, and we worked it out ahead.

Why not have a birthday party and invite others, or get a Sunday picnic together after church? Ask a few who never get invitations.

Others will follow your example and reach out when they see the unlovely or weak ones responding to your love.

Sometimes I took the girls out and had tea with them. Other times we organized a sleep over. We've never had a television, so we were used to games and visiting for our fun. The important thing seemed to be giving Tanya the sense that she was important and that I cared enough to put her first in our relationship.

Jesus called the children over and held them up to everybody as examples of God's kingdom. God has great things for every one of our children. Our part is to point our children to Him. We need to show them who their Heavenly Father really is.

Too many single parents think they can't make it on their own. So the children get left out of the ring while the parent frantically looks for another match. But this doesn't need to happen. When we seek God first, He brings everything else to us. But this implies trust!

God promises to be a Father to the fatherless. What a privilege! To help a child know the very intimate fatherhood of God!

Oscar Wilde's pessimistic fate still falls on those kids not guided into a personal salvation. He said that children begin by loving their parents. As the children grow older, they judge the parents and sometimes they forgive them.

What a pity! No tears or regrets will save a child who never knew God. On the other hand, when a child knows God, he receives all the benefits of a perfect Father's love! Even a parent's gaps are filled in by God, so the child can't lose.

And God begins to work in that child's heart, strengthening him and maturing him to cope with what lacks in the home. When Tanya was very young, I was a new Christian and a single parent. I made many mistakes. But God took care of her, all the while growing me into a more mature, loving parent.

The first time I thanked God for filling in gaps in our home was at our devotions one night. After we had the final prayer, Tanya slid her arm into mine and said: "I'm so glad when God was giving out families that He gave you to me."

Even though her words were like the breeze of a warm south wind in winter, I wondered about them. *Why doesn't my 10-year-old ever complain about being an only child in a single-parent home,* I questioned?

One of the men on my high school staff often teased me, "You just wait, Ellen! I've got three teenagers." He didn't need to say anymore. We both knew what he was thinking. When Sandy, his sixteen-year-old, was in my eleventh-grade English class, she skipped school on a regular basis and even ran away to live with friends before the year was up. Then Tim, his youngest, dropped out of school after a fight with his parents and left to travel the gambling circuit with a racing team.

But I was always convinced we could hope for more if we prayed for our children and committed them totally to God daily. I was not prepared to accept the world's harsh ways for my daughter. What I didn't understand was how to help a teen through those rather tough years with love and wisdom. When the problems came for the first time, I saw where many Christian parents give up. My own experience opened my eyes to see how easy it is to drive our teens away at the very time we need each other most.

Tanya and I had found ourselves alone when she was two. There were many things we had to work through to make life run at even half-mast for the first few years. When our friends went off on holidays, we often spring-cleaned for instance. The days never seemed to stretch long enough to pile English teaching, homework, preparation, and domestic routines into one.

It took many months before I began to realize that the pressures of job and home would not be minimized until I set more priorities. So, when I saw this, I sat down and reorganized my week. Only this time I put Tanya over cleaning cupboards and ironing. Somehow, once we got the order straight, the other fell into place. And we were much happier.

We rearranged our day to better suit my busy high-school teaching schedule. Laundry times often didn't come until after 11:00 P.M. More than once I found myself out buying sandwich meat after midnight at the convenience store a dozen blocks from our little home.

On Saturday we avoided all the things regular working parents might do, like cleaning and car repairs, and we just spent the day together. Sometimes we went for a hike that lasted the whole day, or we visited someone special in our church family. The main branch of our library often found us searching out our favorite reading materials, or we'd have friends over to be part of our day. A big emphasis was spent on listening to where the other person was coming from.

Then on a cold night we curled up by the fire with a good book and thanked God for His many blessings on our home. It seemed that we had a line of openness that was rare, if some of the other stories we heard were true. We often thanked God for giving grace to us to be close.

Then one day . . . Presto! Everything changed. "Clean your room Tanya, please," became the bottom line of every conversation! "Did you have your devotions this morning?" was a close second.

It seemed so reasonable to tell Tanya to do this and don't do that. But something was wrong. Tanya was reacting!

Why was Tanya not responding anymore? Worse still, why was she resentful? And when we were together for longer periods of time, why did we needle each other? We both felt it and asked each other why? I almost gave in and accepted most of my friends' opinions. "Tanya is a teen now," and everybody knows that teens are just "different," so we can expect tension under some pressures. But just in time, I began to pray about it; I asked God to show me why this was happening, and what I should do.

I knew the problem was not that we were holding too tightly. We both felt strongly about letting others into our hearts and lives and not making our love exclusive. *Then could it be a teenage rebellion problem?* I questioned. But Tanya is not rebellious. She has a heart bigger than mine by far. That couldn't be it!

One Saturday afternoon on a long bus ride, things came to a head. "Lord," I prayed, "we love each other so much. Will You help us to run to You right now and clear whatever this barrier is?" At that moment I could not kneel and repent without the whole bus being in on the action, so I closed my eyes and pictured myself kneeling in front of Jesus with no answers or solutions, rather desperate. "Please direct me, Lord," I prayed. Peace filled my heart, and I knew that God wanted me to say I was sorry for any conflict. I told Him I was sorry, and then I asked Tanya to forgive me. She did. I still had no solution, but I had my joy back when we rolled into the terminal, and so did Tanya.

In the next few days the Lord continued to answer my prayer. I wanted to get to the bottom of the stirring in our relationship and deal with the roots. Again the root of the problem was me! God is so gracious to teach us and to love us through everything when we let go. Once I had the thing by the handle I knew we were all right.

Our main hurdle was this: I was still relating to Tanya as if she was the little girl I have always known. I was doing too much of the suggesting and too little listening. I simply had too many easy answers to her life without giving Tanya the right to find them in her own way. I was too unbendable in my thoughts for her upbringing. She was very willing to change and was looking for a framework to grow in: I had chisled it down too narrow. She couldn't get through. So she was cornered.

Teenagers are not ten-year-olds or even twelve-year-olds; they are on the brink of being men and women. Mary was probably barely a teen when she gave birth to Jesus! Our teens deserve to see their parents being molded and shaped by God and not to have all the answers passed to them in microwave fashion. If we let Him, God will use our teenagers to teach us how to love others in a deeper way.

Children often learn God's ways more by watching and participating. Even more than by just listening to a parent preach. I used to give long sermons on many issues. Every situation had its answer in Scripture I decided. So I put Tanya through the rigors of hearing the Scriptural side of everything she or I did. We all know that Scripture does have every answer. But where I fell short was method.

"Children have more need of models than of critics," Joseph Joubert said.

Becoming good role models does not imply being perfect. Far from it! But I found that by admitting my weakness openly and saying: "I'm sorry," I strengthened ties. Kids always respect an adult who will humble themselves and ask forgiveness. Let's face it. Pride yells: "No, you don't have to!" So I had to remind myself often. With no partners to play referee, a single parent is on his own honor here.

Bible Study Suggestions

1 Samuel 2; Jeremiah 1; Romans 8:14-15; Psalm 68:5-6;

Practical Applications

1. How did God use Samuel at an early age and work with him?

2. How old was Jeremiah when God began to use him mightily in prophecy?

3. Describe each of your children as you feel the Lord sees them.

4. Ask the Lord to help you guide each one into His plans for their lives right now. Discuss these points with the child in your next Bible study and prayer time.

5. How can you bring God's unity to the family when there is one parent? Look at Psalm 68:5-6.

6. What does it mean to your family to be adopted into God's family? See Romans 8:14-15.

7. Have each child write a letter to their Heavenly Father, telling Him about their needs and their love for Him. Make these letters an object for prayer, unless they are personal and would be better not shared. Be sensitive here.

13
No Need to Be Superparent

Even the most stalwart among us find the pressures of single parenting staggering at times. Not one of us finds carrying all the burdens that go with it easy. And there are casualties.

I did learn a valuable lesson. You can ride over anxiety's storms when you mount up on eagle's wings. Why bother, you may ask, when frustrations "mount up" instead? But there's something to be said for pressure's unique ability to carry you into a loftier place. And then, like the expert strapped into a hang glider on a calm day, you look at the forest from another perspective.

I discovered God not only gives strength for my weariness but adds power to my weakness. And all while I rest in Him! Remember His promise:

> He gives strength to the weary
> and increases the power of the weak.
> Even youths grow tired and weary,
> and young men stumble and fall;
> but those who hope in the Lord
> will renew their strength.
> They will soar on wings like eagles;
> they will run and not grow weary,
> they will walk and not be faint (Isa. 40:29-31).

Even from the quicksands of loneliness and despair you can actually mount eagle's wings and fly over the problems. What does that mean for the single parent, you may ask? Consider the facts!

The eagle flies as high as 6,000 feet while sustaining its position. To soar on its wings is to rest on the strength of the Holy Spirit and allow Him to hold us in that lofty place in God. When we ride on His wings, we see everything from God's perspective. We can see as the eagle does with a bird's-eye view. Did you ever look at a screen out of focus and then watch the lines around each object sharpen until the whole scene became clear. The pieces fit together when you look through God's eyes. Things make sense.

If you're like me you sometimes feel like the three-year-old girl who when asked to give thanks at lunch prayed: "Thanks for the cows that give milk. Thanks for the chickens that give eggs. And thanks for the Campbells that give soup." Do you ever get your syllogisms wrong? Every time you do, your conclusion will be off, too. That's why the Holy Spirit promised to help you in your weakness in Romans 8:26.

No longer do we have to strive with the limited view of the disjointed and disunited parts, trying to make them all fit. We learn to look from this vantage place with the eyes of our faith rather than mere natural vision.

We can refuse to look at a thing with earth's perspective and choose to soar up, letting our wings beat the upper air, as the eagle does. I had a hard time getting past my feelings. When they were negative, I sank. One day a dear friend I often get advice from told me, "Your feelings have nothing to do with reality." She reminded me, "God's love for you is perfect because He died to make you righteous. His love never depends on your feelings." Once I learned this I found negative feelings dropped away faster.

Remember, eagles are concerned with mountains, not molehills; canyons, not mud puddles. They swoop over lofty heights and great canyons with the same majestic ease. And so can you!

The Holy Spirit has a place of wonderful destiny for those who will come. It should humble one to compare this life with that of scratching around on the ground pecking for a few seeds. There should be no pride here, as there is no self-attainment. But God takes each one who will mount up to discover the depth, magnitude, and mystery of His plan for our lives.

Just like the eagle, the most solitary of any bird, the single parent often travels alone with God. There is a time when God wants to isolate His children, even call them into the wilderness, so He can teach them the higher path of love and trust.

There is a certain quietness that accompanies the person who is led through a wilderness experience with God. Just as the eagle—that quiet, determined bird—soars freely, so can you. Put your trust in God to take you through the tough experience of each trial. Then soar. You can walk quietly as Jesus did in the face of accusations, loneliness, hardships, and misunderstanding when you know He carries you. But to appropriate this strength, you must take to the upper air like the eagle, alone and yielded to God's ability to carry you.

Not until I watched a young eagle riding on the wings of the wind, high above the storm clouds on the Grand Canyon, did I see why God speaks so much about eagles in the Bible.

The comparison is especially encouraging for the parent struggling alone. Eagles symbolize our own calling. Only those who "mount up" will ever know the joy of being caught up to the throne of God, molded into His image to rule and reign with Him forever!

I was often more like a chicken at first. I was earthbound, never lifting my sight above the ground. One only has to get bound up within fences, squabbling greedily for a little feed someone might throw in, to crave the higher calling of the eagle.

Just like the eagle, we have to soar high, in wide open spaces into the clouds in heaven to see freedom and excitement. It will probably be lonely there at first. It almost seems more natural to stay below and complain about the rough life you have. But those who soar will never want to come back to that.

I remember the fear I felt when no financial help came from my broken marriage. It would have been so much easier at first to go to court like others advised. But God taught me a better way, and He has provided for all my needs over thirteen years. How much easier it is to trust Him for the future now that He has allowed me to soar over my fear and see His faithfulness!

But eagles in the Christian life don't grow to be mature eagles overnight. Look at Deuteronomy 32:10-11 to see the way a young eagle learns to fly in comparison to God's child:

> In a desert land he found him,
> in a barren and howling waste.
> He shielded him and cared for him;
> he guarded him as the apple of his eye,
> like an eagle that stirs up its next
> and hovers over its young,
> that spreads its wings to catch them
> and carries them on its pinions.

Don't be alarmed when things that were easy now become hard. It may be God nudging you off your comfortable cliffs onto higher plains. He will catch you before you fall.

I found God tested me many times to show me what still croached dormant in my heart. I thought I had learned how to forgive, for example, until a Christian woman deliberately left me off the list of a party for my friend because I was a single parent. Anger and hurt feelings hung over me like a storm cloud for days! Then I saw it. God allowed this to lift some old habits to the surface. How freeing it was to say: "Forgive me, Lord, and thank You for showing me the deception of my own heart."

The very storms that huddle chickens together in fright challenge the eagle to go higher. Lifted above the fury of the lightning and thunderbolts, he glides almost effortless after a time. With keen vision he prospers where a lower creature perishes.

God adds vision to the one who rises above earthly limitations to take hold of the eagle's view. While others perish for lack of vision (Prov. 29:18), the eagle-minded person penetrates the height and depths of God's mind for that situation.

It is much easier to be comfortable. That is why God sometimes has to take us out of that broken nest. The mother eagle actually beats her young with her wings. Those same wings the eaglet once scurried under for protection seem to rise up against him. The little eaglet climbs to the side of the nest to escape the flutter of her big wings.

This allows the mother to spread her wings, and the eaglet to hop onto her back for the first lesson. The nest is no longer safe to hold the growing babies. At first, the ride becomes a thrilling adventure. But when they are high into the clouds the mother darts out from under her young eagle, leaving him nothing to hang onto.

She ignores his screams for help as he tumbles down, instinctively flapping his wings in panic bursts and fear. When the mother sees her baby's wings fail to support him, she swoops back under. What relief for the little fellow! Just before he crashes into the rocks below, he is rescued.

Back up into the heights the little one goes, secure on his mother's strong sure back, but only to begin the process again. Once he is rested and the height is gained, the bottom drops away again until eventually the young bird's little wings catch the currents of air, and he takes flight on his own. Only then will the young eagle enjoy the higher view, the majestic sails of a heavenly flight.

There was a period in my single-parent walk when I would not mount up and allow God to take me through. This brought trouble. I complained about the load at school, fought against the weight at home, and made misery a welcome child in our family. The result was havoc.

Secular books told me to be "Supermom," and I gave it my best shot. My pride smarted when we failed, so I raised my expectations and set out to ace them. When one of my colleagues at the high school told me I was pushing it too hard, I defended single parents across the whole universe. I even sent Tanya to school with a high fever one day because "supermoms" don't call in when a child is ill. They push on.

Then one day my back simply gave out. It began to spasm, and every movement made me scream with pain. I called in sick and telephoned my pastor and his wife, who are dear friends. When they picked me up and collected a few items to take to their home with us, I could not even walk to the car.

My condition lasted one month. There I lay, too crippled to sit, stand, or walk. The doctor came by every few days at first and then once a week until I could walk without spasms. But I learned to let God take me through my tough places into higher plains during that month. I let go and let God, for the first time ever.

Not only did I learn to soar like an eagle, but I entered into God's promise for His weary children. Over and over, my meditation brought me back to the psalm of David while I was bedridden:

> The Lord is my shepherd, I shall lack nothing.
>> He makes me lie down in green pastures,
> he leads me beside quiet waters,
>> he restores my soul.
> He guides me in paths of righteousness
>> for his name's sake.
> Even though I walk
>> through the valley of the shadow of death,
> I will fear no evil,
>> for you are with me;
> your rod and your staff,
>> they comfort me.
>
> You prepare a table before me
>> in the presence of my enemies.
> You annoint my head with oil;
>> my cup overflows.
> Surely goodness and love will follow me
>> all the days of my life,

and I will dwell in the house of the Lord
   forever (23:1-6).

There have been other times where God dropped bottoms out of my independent plans to teach me His higher ways. I remember one occasion where I was the conference speaker at a major Christian teachers' convention. One of the parents who felt church doctrines rather than Bible should be taught in the classroom traveled many miles to come and hear my talk. After weeks of diligent preparation and hours of setting up displays, I jumped into my sessions with all the energy I could muster. Encouraged by the positive response of the many teachers to the topics, I felt pleased with the whole event.

Later, I discovered this parent went back to my board and wrote one of the strongest letters against a person's teaching I've ever heard. After fifteen years of teaching, I was undone!

Through it all, God taught me how to ride eagle wings in violent storms and leave the other elements to Him. When I meet this dear older man today, I can look him in the eye with Christian love. I know that he was the very tool God chose to teach me a more valuable truth than I could learn at a teachers' convention.

Tanya and I are more confident now in His saving ability and less confident in our own efforts. There have been big victories. And we remember many failures.

But each time He swooped down and picked us up before we hit sharp objects below. And each time He left us with our wings stronger to beat against the currents of air in that higher flight.

Bible Study Suggestions

Matthew 23:12; 2 Cor 12:5-12; Philippians 2:3-11;

Practical Applications

1. What does Jesus say about His own response to our pride? (Matt. 23:12).

2. What does Paul say about his own weaknesses? Look at 2 Corinthians 12:5-12.

3. Tell how Jesus makes Himself weak? (Phil. 2:3-11).

4. What weaknesses do you have?

5. List your strengths?

6. How can the Lord use both? Be specific.

14
A Small Support Group

Have you ever prayed: "O, Lord, Your waters are so vast, and my vessel so small"? I have. Maybe you give everything you have but the kids still need more. Or your boss asks you at the last minute to stay on, and the baby-sitter has already threatened to quit the next time you arrive late. Your head starts to throb, and you want to disappear into another world—evaporate. Perhaps that's what Jonathan Edwards meant when he said that nothing is what sleeping rocks dream about.

It's then a person needs a support group. Just a few who can enter into the rough seas, or the cold storm, makes all the difference. A support group helps people hang in when they want to give up.

The day my friend's seven-year-old daughter, Tracey, traded her baseball glove for a bantam rooster, she brought the thing home, and it stuck its head into the dog's mouth. So every time the dog yawned, it closed its mouth on the chicken until my friend sent all three outside and called our house for any suggestions. The fact is, everybody needs somebody at times like these.

A support group could be a small Bible study group, a home fellowship group, or a prayer group. But it should be smaller than a congregation and bigger than blood relatives. Jesus had a circle He turned to.

One of the blessings of God's family is that there is room for everybody. It distressed Jesus to see people scattered, alone:

When he saw the crowds, he had compassion on them, because they
were harassed and helpless, like sheep without a shepherd. (Matt.
9:36).

Homogeneous groups don't usually work as well as groups con-
sisting of all ages, all backgrounds. Such a variety lends character
and vitality to the whole.

The early church operated through home groups. Today we
have the added joy of coming together with the larger body for
times of worship, teaching, and sharing.

Singles and single parents often have no place to drop in for
coffee and a chat. They may be without any support system or place
to call. There were days when I came in from high school too
exhausted to cook dinner and hit the marking. One night I called
a sister from my group and suggested we have dinner together once
a month, and take turns making it. She thought it was a great idea,
and my dilemma was solved. This took care of the sometimes—
painful sting of singleness that comes when the chips are down
through work loads.

Then there are the older saints! What a blessing they are to have
in the group. How else can you hear the stories of the First World
War, early revivals, or hayrides through the country on a fall
evening? Yet this section of the body of Christ gets left out in the
mad rush of today's world. They no longer have chores on the farm
and skills to pass down to their grandchildren. They do have
treasures to pass along.

You might say they keep things more in perspective. I used to
long for the revivals I read about to come again. Somehow I figured
we'd all love more, church would become angelic, and God would
always be there. "The only secure part is God in any revival," said
one woman in her nineties. She told me how men were even more
foolish sometimes when revivals hit. "Billy Sunday, that great
preacher, got so excited during one meeting," she said. "He leaped
up onto the podium and started waving a chair at the people,

shouting about their shortcomings. His wife, twice the size of Billy, ran up to the front of the church, grabbed him by the pant leg and yelled, 'Billy, you get down right now!' " My myths were shattered, and I saw that only God is perfect. Even during the greatest movements we've known, man is simply man. But it took an older saint to show me that.

My daughter never knew the joy of grandparents until her adopted Grandpa and Grandma Mitchell took her under their wing. She brags about them now like any other kid brags about somebody who really cares. And so do I. There is no time day or night that I am not welcome to drop in on Bob and Ruth. If relatives arrive, we all eat together. But it remains a home where the family of God can join under a loving roof when they need to feel the closeness of other members. That is the first such home I've known. But God used it to demonstrate His love over and over.

And there were other places. Dick and Anne Spicer always have a warm hug and tea for those who come by, and the Davidsons quickly make anybody part of their family activity. Tanya's godparents, John and Eva, always find time and love for others.

There will be setbacks. Jealousy and rebellion might even try to slip in like little foxes. Remember though, run to God when jealousy threatens. My own prayer is: "Father, keep me humble, so my heart will always be satisfied in You." But there is always a way for those who look to Christ together. These problems can be the very stepping-stones to a higher place for the threatened relationship. What hurts more is the thought somebody else might be jealous of me. God is a great God, and we are His children, but we are mere sinners saved by grace. My responsibility toward others is to prefer them above myself whenever I can. This calls for humility on my part every time and short accounts. But it works! You may even lose kindred friends when jealousy strikes but run to God, and you find a Friend who will never turn away.

We must be willing to grow and change. God will never force us. But I found that if I just hang in, He brings beauty from every ash. And I believe God still sends grandparents to kids who have none. In fact, I know some old folks who brag about dozens of grandkids they adopted over the years. When my own grandmother visited me as I child, I felt safe and warm because she was there. She brought the yesterdays of home-baked apple pie, custom-knit slippers, and a friendly hug.

You might say, "But today's granny is a chic career woman. She probably dashes off to Arizona for the winter months, drinks diet colas, and lives in a retirement village that's off-limits to children."

Your own children can draw the generations closer, and they once again discover the magic that spills from an older woman's hands onto a child's.

Since I don't remember either grandfather, I simply adopted one. It just seemed logical my best friend's grandpa could be mine at the same time. I still remember one afternoon we picked raspberries together for dinner. And Grandpa told me something I'll never forget. "Don't be afraid to be friendly, Ellen," he said. "Everybody's really kinfolk." And whenever I think of kinfolk today, somebody who kind of shines from the ordinary, I think of how Grandpa treated you like his own so you felt it deep inside.

Somebody said: "Christianity is a blast when you go God's way!" I love to fellowship with people who enjoy Christ as much as I do. He has a challenge around every corner when we walk on!

When E. W. Howe said: "Some men storm imaginary Alps all their lives and die in the foothills cursing difficulties that do not exist" (from *Success Easier than Failures*), he was probably looking at people who try to answer every question on their own.

But others can bring a dimension into the hurdle that beams light on a hidden angle. Our part is to listen. Ralph Waldo Emerson said: "There is guidance for each of us, and by lowly listening, we shall hear the right word."

That word has often come to me in a dry moment or a time of struggling with loneliness. It has come through friends, elders, young children, and peers. When it has been from God, there is a lifting off of some burden or a light in my tunnel to see me through.

And often the word comes in the most natural ways. While taking a walk with a friend one day, she began to share with me her advice to another young lady. The Holy Spirit was taking that older woman's words and planting them as encouragement in my own heart. So I went home assured that I did not have to earn God's love, that grace was a free gift and was God's help to me in every situation. I was facing a tough financial battle and felt condemned. It seemed that God was far away. But those words brought life and new courage to walk on.

Often we only need to be told: "Hold God's hand and walk on!" That is enough. It gets us up out of the dust of self-pity, or the temptation to run away, and moves us another step with Christ at our side.

There were times when others gave me strong advice that left me feeling weighted down. The job seemed too big. I was unarmed for it. Later I discovered some of these words of advice went against God's Word. God is never a taskmaster. His yoke is easy and His burden light.

Often others confirm what we already feel is the right direction. This can be very assuring since there is no partner to share ideas or plans with. Just talking it out, listening actively, and forming a plan of attack is all that's needed often.

I often felt guilty about what I didn't do or was not. Through the counsel of others I saw that whenever I am troubled with a feeling of guilt, I cannot be for the moment all that I am capable of. Guilt kind of drains me. Pushing guilt away was never effective. I learned to identify it and go for the cause. What a relief to be free of weight that God never intended I carry.

Another area I needed help for was depression. When things went wrong, or when others let me down, I got depressed. It took some time for me to understand the process. For a long time I had to ignore my feelings about a thing and keep busy doing just exactly what God wanted me to do in spite of how I felt. I sat down one day and made a full list of the things I neglected to do because I didn't feel like doing them. Then I asked God to forgive my neglect. Sometimes, I had to confess negative thoughts about another person also before things bounced back to normal. But through my support group, and through the Lord's grace, I was able to kill the monster—depression—before self-pity followed him in. What a victory!

Keep busy doing God's work when you want to give up, and you'll find God keeps busy taking care of your needs whatever they are. That key helped me over and over. It really comes down to obedience. When I listen to God and obey, I'll avoid the traps I fall into when I'm running my own race.

There were others in my group who usually needed help. So when I felt discouraged, I prayed for them or phoned them. Even when I reached out, I found God's comfort back to me was more than enough to carry me through any hard place.

And don't be afraid of taking your masks off. Some may criticize you, a few may turn away, but most will find it easier to be real themselves if you start. Hold onto God's unconditional love though. It will hold you up if somebody lets you down. For years I did not understand that even when a person I loved turned away, I could be secure inside. When I discovered this, forgiveness became a whole lot easier. And I no longer condemned myself when I failed others. Instead I had the confidence to ask their forgiveness and then go on.

Kind words are often much more important to give to others than advice, I found. Do you see an oak when you look at an acorn? God did when He made it. And we can, too. When I try to change somebody else, especially if that person wears a handicap up front, I may miss the treasure I could have unwrapped in that person. But when I look at those God led into my life as His dear children, I speak differently. Have you ever noticed how you run faster toward love than harsh words. Not one of us are put into each other's circles because we're perfect. But we are put there because God wanted each one to teach the other. When I saw this, I became more careful with the lives of those around me. I am committed to those God sends, no matter who they are.

Bible Study Suggestions

1 Thessalonians 3:7-8; Matthew 15:32; Hosea 11:1-3; Luke 15:19-20;

Practical Applications

1. How did Paul treat those in his care? (1 Thess. 3:7-8).

2. How did Jesus react to the groups He worked with? (Matt. 15:32).

3. What is God's thought about extended family? (Hos. 11:1-3).

4. How did Jesus treat a family member who made foolish mistakes? (Luke 15:19-20).

15
Delight Yourself in the Lord

Did you ever wake up on top of the world one day and in the bottom of a narrow trench the next? Your feelings shout, "You'll be famous!" when you're up, and, "You're a fool!" when you hit the dust. Not one of us can avoid some measure of those emotional swings. I found, however, my own little family provides a sheltering tree in the storms and cool shade in the heat, a tree that lets me stand firm and put my own roots down beside it.

So, who does that include? you might ask. In my case the number varies. Tanya, my daughter provides me daily with what I call "a living picture of God's grace." She has taught me more about love than any other human, and I trust her. We have a very special relationship, and a deep friendship. And that's been going on since day one. We've weathered the storms together, and we've clung to God when waves rocked our home. We've trusted Him together and laughed through the unconventional systems we often created to survive my crazy schedules.

One of the strongest bonds in our home is open communication. No games. You say what you need to and then work it through in prayer with God's help.

Others I consider family are those very few special people you can just be yourself with. And the ebb and flow of these few into our lives comprise family. You let them closer, because they love you. They speak reality into your world, acting as sandpaper when you chip or splinter and a buffer when you're alone. Remember

137

how the Lord picked His family: those who "received his word" (Acts 2:41, KJV). And we, too, choose.

I find He sends just the right ones. One Christmas we adopted an older lady off the street, and today we are still good friends because God opened our eyes to Marian's worth.

A philosopher once said: "Know thyself." And since it is impossible to know ourselves outside of God, we need to go to Him as a family as well as individuals. Then we see ourselves as we really are—our characters, motives, attitudes, and actions.

You can be sure conflicts will confront every family and its extension, though. But when a person looks into the mirror of God's Word to find answers, self-justification in family matters falls away. Faults are uncovered by the power of the Word and then cleansed in its wake. In other words, people love you as you are and never turn away when you fail, but you are safe enough to be real. That kind of communication can only survive in a family that looks to God, not traditions or "common sense" for vital answers.

Our deeply rooted natural tendency is to explain away our faults or blame another member in the family. But coming together daily and submitting to God's Word challenges a person to personal honesty and humility, then one can accept one's shortcomings and ask forgiveness.

Someone once said: "The only difference between stumbling blocks and stepping-stones is in how you use them." In times of Bible study and prayer we turn everyday hurdles into challenges. This is only possible with God.

Let's face it. Single parenting is tough. But I can refuse to let troubles caused by this life block my path. One day, after God has breathed new life on my built-in stumbling-blocks, I will be able to say as did Tennyson in "In Memoriam":

> Men may rise on stepping-stones
> Of their dead selves to higher things.

Create an atmosphere of acceptance and love around the study of God's Word. Never use the Word as a bludgeon for children, or you will defeat its bigger power. God's Word is one of love, and He never departs from love, even when He disciplines a child.

The Word will do a work as it is applied, meditated on, prayed over, and discussed. Each one in the group might ask: How can I change today in light of the Word we studied? Let God be the one to make the changes!

As difficult as it may be, we have to face our faults and guard against self-justification before we can be changed. How often have I made excuses for myself or blamed my misfortunes on others? It was meditation and study of God's Word that showed me this fatal error.

As single persons, we throw ourselves harder onto God for guidance because there is usually nobody else to check us or help us. When we run to God with the family, He becomes central to the family's everyday lives. How often Tanya and I reminded ourselves in those times that God was our Father and my husband. It was a great comfort to us as we finally began to live with this assurance. Before this we often felt alone and even deserted.

While Tanya was young I had devotions with her each day, but always with a mind to guiding her into her own walk with God. I knew that she would never come into a relationship with Him on my coattails. Also, she had many gifts and talents I didn't have. So I tried not to impose my own walk on my daughter.

In the school where I taught for ten years I saw many teens walk away from God as soon as they grew old enough to slide out of their parent's grip. The problem was that no personal walk with God held them. The parents might have known the Lord, but the kids never did. Not only that, these kids were never asked to choose God's way. So when they got old enough, they chose the wide gate. It is easier to go the way of your peers and have fun than submit yourself to God.

The parents were devastated and wondered how this could have happened. "We always had Bible times together," they often told me. But this is not enough strength to take a child through the tough hurdles of today's society. Each one of us needs to be born again and come to know Jesus as our personal Savior.

Family devotions propel you and your children into God's stream of life daily. Before the mountains overwhelm me, I have the strength and insight to walk through them one at a time.

> A little consideration of what takes place around us every day, would show us that a higher law than that of our will, regulates events; that our painful experiences are not necessary. A believing love will relieve us of a vast load of care. Oh, my brothers, God exists!
>
> —Ralph Waldo Emerson

Those big stumbling blocks that a family member often carries alone become stepping-stones when shared with others in God's presence. If there is a school problem, talk it over. Find an example in Scripture where a way out follows. Pray about God's direction on the matter. Not only will you leave with the joy of His direction, but the very thing that weighted one person down becomes the tool that unifies a family.

Each one will become stronger, strengthening the family bond at the same time when a family comes to God to improve matters for everyone concerned. The main one to change, I found, was me. Not my circumstances or my life: *me!*

> Maturity is the capacity to withstand ego-destroying experiences, and not lose one's perspective in the ego-building experiences.
>
> —Robert K. Greenleaf

Our prayer and Bible study sets the stage for witnessing Christ to others. We make sure to pray for the ones God indicates to us. Then we make it a project to visit or help those in need.

There is a great joy in blessing others in Christ as a family. I believe that God wants us to reach out with our families to draw others in as we are able.

It is here that children learn by example how to love others deeply. It is here they learn to give and put others first. But there will be opposition!

We could count on telephones ringing, doorbells clanging, and every other distraction as soon as we got together for devotions. Once I realized this was a deliberate attempt of the enemy to prevent God's work, I took steps to eliminate those tactics. We let the telephone ring, and unless the door situation was an emergency, we asked people to wait.

It is in family devotions that kids learn warfare. We took hard situations in our own lives and prayed that God would give us the strength to walk through. Remembering it was through suffering Jesus that Himself was perfected (Heb. 2:10), I was careful not to ask to be delivered from every tough place. Instead we asked for the strength to say thank you for each thing God sent for that day, and the grace to overcome!

We often began our next devotions with discussion on the last day's progress. This practice establishes a discipline in children that will turn them to Christ in every difficulty they encounter. Even when you are not there they will know who to run to and who they can depend on.

Praise is an important part of our devotions. If nobody plays an instrument, use a tape and just worship the Lord with it. Somebody said, "Don't worry about the way your voice sounds. God makes it beautiful before it reaches heaven anyway."

By praising God we learned how to praise Him throughout the day on our own. It was easier to sing a praise song to Him in the car in the afternoon when we met Him with one that morning. And sometimes we remembered to praise Him when we didn't feel like it later in the day. A regular practice will eventually become a habit.

Above all, we learned to enjoy God's presence together. And He taught us how to hang in when things went badly. We discussed the answers He gave to our prayers and explored ways to meditate and study the Scriptures effectively. And we recorded answers when they came. And they did!

Each year we prayed about Tanya's school, and each year God made it clear where He wanted her and then provided the way. When she reached grade nine, the tuition climbed well out of my reach. We prayed and cried together, deciding to tell nobody but God about our plight. Then two weeks before school opened we had a call from the school saying an anonymous donor came by and paid for her year. And we knew that once again His fatherhood had visited our single parent home in a tangible way. And if He says no to our prayers, we have learned to look beyond the instant disappointment to God's constant faithfulness over our little family since the day we first gave Him our trust. Over and over our Friend and Savior, Christ, proved: we may be a single-parent family, but He is with us in everything. *We are never alone.*

Bible Study Suggestions

Deuteronomy 4:9-10; 1 Corinthians 16:19; 1 Chronicles 22:13

Practical Applications

1. What does God say about His Word in families? (Deut. 4:9-10).

2. Does the Bible say that a family must have devotions together? (1 Cor. 16:19).

3. What does God promise each one who studies and keeps His Word? (1 Chron. 22:13).